Developmentally Appropriate Practice

Focus on
INFANTS AND TODDLERS

Carol Copple, Sue Bredekamp,
Derry Koralek, and Kathy Charner, editors

National Association for the Education of Young Children
Washington, DC

National Association for the
Education of Young Children
1313 L Street NW, Suite 500
Washington, DC 20005-4101
202-232-8777 • 800-424-2460
www.naeyc.org

NAEYC Books

Chief Publishing Officer
Derry Koralek

Editor-in-Chief
Kathy Charner

Director of Creative Services
Edwin C. Malstrom

Managing Editor
Mary Jaffe

Senior Editor
Holly Bohart

Senior Graphic Designer
Malini Dominey

Associate Editor
Elizabeth Wegner

Editorial Assistant
Ryan Smith

Through its publications program, the National Association
for the Education of Young
Children (NAEYC) provides
a forum for discussion of
major issues and ideas in the
early childhood field, with the
hope of provoking thought
and promoting professional
growth. The views expressed
or implied in this book are
not necessarily those of the
Association or its members.

Photo Credits

Copyright © Julia Luckenbill: cover (right, and third and fourth on
left), interior cover (upper left, upper right, and bottom), 3, 8, 15, 18,
23, 31, 35, 39, 43, 97, 98, 101, 104, 109, 115, 148; Ellen B. Senisi: cover
(second on left), 44, 47, 49, 94, 95, 99; Jude Keith Rose: 12; Marilyn
Nolt: 93

Copyright © NAEYC: cover (top left), interior cover (center), 106

Courtesy of the *Young Children* article's authors: 105, 107, 110, 113,
117, 118, 119, 120, 122, 130, 131, 133, 137, 138, 139, 140, 143, 145

Contributing editor: *Steve Olle*

Library of Congress Control Number: 2013936366
ISBN: 978-1-928896-95-1
NAEYC Item #168

Contents

About the Editors

Carol Copple is a highly respected early childhood education author, educator, and consultant. For 16 years she served as a senior staff member at NAEYC, and her responsibilities included directing the books program. She has taught at Louisiana State University and the New School for Social Research, and she codeveloped and directed a research-based model for preschool education at the Educational Testing Service. With Sue Bredekamp, Carol is coeditor of *Developmentally Appropriate Practice in Early Childhood Programs* (1997; 2009). Among her other books are *Learning to Read and Write: Developmentally Appropriate Practices for Young Children* (NAEYC); *Growing Minds: Building Strong Cognitive Foundations in Early Childhood* (NAEYC); and *Educating the Young Thinker: Classroom Strategies for Cognitive Growth* (Lawrence Erlbaum). She received her doctorate from Cornell University.

Sue Bredekamp is an early childhood education specialist from Washington, DC. She serves as a consultant on developmentally appropriate practice, curriculum, teaching, and professional development for many state and national organizations, including NAEYC, the Council for Professional Recognition, Head Start, and Sesame Workshop. From 1981 to 1998, she was director of accreditation and professional development for NAEYC. Sue is the primary author of the 1987 edition of *Developmentally Appropriate Practice in Early Childhood Programs*, and coeditor (with Carol Copple) of the 1997 and 2009 revisions. She is the author of the introductory textbook *Effective Practices in Early Childhood Education: Building a Foundation, 2nd Edition* (Pearson). Sue was a member of the National Research Council's Committee on Early Childhood Mathematics, and she holds a PhD in curriculum and instruction from the University of Maryland.

Derry Koralek, chief publishing officer of NAEYC, oversees the development of all print and digital publishing, including books, brochures, periodicals, professional development guides, posters, and websites for educators and families. Derry is editor in chief of *Young Children* and *TYC—Teaching Young Children*.

Kathy Charner is editor in chief of NAEYC's Books and Related Resources department, with responsibility for the content, management, publication, and general excellence of the books and brochures published by NAEYC. Before joining NAEYC, Kathy was editor in chief at Gryphon House for more than 20 years.

Acknowledgments

This book—and the NAEYC position statement on developmentally appropriate practice it is based on—reflects the expertise and experience of a great many people working in early childhood education over the years. These individuals have deepened our collective knowledge and understanding of young children through their work with young children and study of early childhood teaching and learning.

In 2006 NAEYC launched a discussion among early childhood professionals to inform the revision of its 1996 position statement. Internet technology made it possible for a wider group of people to participate in the discussion than was ever possible previously. The revision process included a thorough review of current research; open forums at NAEYC conferences; convening of a DAP Working Group to advise on content and to review and revise drafts; input, review, and comment by NAEYC Affiliate Groups and pertinent professional organizations; public invitation to anyone in the field to comment on the draft via NAEYC's website; and finally, consideration and approval by NAEYC's Governing Board.

Space prevents us from acknowledging all of the contributions, but we must mention the following:

The outstanding members of the 2007 DAP Working Group. This delightful, knowledgeable group (Juanita Copley, Carolyn Pope Edwards, Linda Espinosa, Ellen Frede, Mary Louise Hemmeter, Marjorie Kostelnik, and Dorothy Strickland) began their work on the position statement revision in March 2007 and continued to respond to that document and plans for the book as they evolved.

The 2007 group's predecessors, the members of NAEYC's Panel on Revisions to Developmentally Appropriate Practice (1993–1996), who gave tirelessly of their time and wisdom to the conceptualization of the 1996 version of the position statement. And before them, the members of NAEYC's 1985 Commission on Appropriate Education for 4- and 5-Year-Olds, who began the process of codifying the Association's position on quality in early childhood practice that culminated in the first position statements on developmentally appropriate practice in 1985/6.

Members of the NAEYC Governing Board (2006–08) for their useful input and much appreciated support.

The NAEYC State Affiliates, who were valuable partners in our collective thinking about developmentally appropriate practice. The Affiliate Council highlighted DAP during their face-to-face meetings, and State Affiliates engaged in strategic discussions with their local member communities, forwarding their responses, questions, and suggestions directly to NAEYC. In addition, several State Affiliates hosted regional discussion groups across their states.

Important feedback provided by leaders of the Southern Early Childhood Association (SECA), which shares NAEYC's commitment to developmentally appropriate practice.

Staff and representatives of ZERO TO THREE, for their work on developmentally appropriate practice for infants and toddlers.

The dozens of early childhood leaders, practitioners, and scholars who reacted to our questions about the position statement revision and then to preliminary drafts. Among the many who helped us in this way, we would like to give special thanks to Elena Bodrova, Barbara Bowman, Mon Cochran, Herb Ginsburg, Deborah Leong, Robert Pianta, Sharon Ritchie, Tom Schultz, Barbara Smith, Dorothy Strickland, Ruby Takanishi, Francis Wardle, and Carol Anne Wien for their thoughtful and detailed comments.

Janet Gonzalez-Mena, who contributed substantively to the book, based on her expertise and wisdom in the areas of infant and toddler care and culture in early care and education.

Gaye Gronlund, project manager for DAP resources and activities for NAEYC.

Of the many supportive colleagues at NAEYC who helped us with the 3rd edition of DAP in so many ways . . .

We especially appreciate the contributions of Linda Halgunseth; Marilou Hyson; Adele Robinson; and the resolute Heather Biggar Tomlinson.

The one indispensable person in this effort from start to finish was the incredible Bry Pollack, nominally the then-managing editor for books but our true partner in every aspect of the work. We are also grateful for the sharp skills, hard work, and unflagging dedication of the other members of the books team, Malini Dominey, Melissa Edwards, and Liz Wegner. And to two of our favorite books department alums, freelance editors Lisa Cook and Natalie Cavanagh.

Thanks to Jerlean Daniel, Mark Ginsberg, Marilyn Smith, and Carol Brunson Day for their personal guidance and consistent support over the years and during our work on the 3rd edition.

   And finally . . .

Special acknowledgment to Patty Smith Hill, Lois Meek Stolz, and Rose Alschuler for their vision, courage, leadership, and commitment in forming an organization that would one day become NAEYC and for framing as its mission the achievement of developmentally appropriate practice in programs for young children.

Editors' Preface

Young children are born learners. Although individual differences are present at birth, most set out to explore their world with unbridled eagerness and curiosity. Perhaps more than any other time of life, early childhood is a period of never ending possibilities. Similarly, most early childhood educators enthusiastically embrace their work, because every day brings the chance to share in children's excitement of discovery. We enter and stay in the field because we believe that our work can make a significant difference in the lives of children and their families, and so make a profound and lasting contribution to society.

But whether we make that difference in young children's lives is not assured. Children are born learners, but for them to actually learn and develop optimally requires us to provide them with care and education of the highest quality. *Developmentally appropriate practice* is a term that has come to be used within the profession to describe the complex and rewarding work done by excellent early childhood educators.

More than 25 years ago, NAEYC published its first position statements defining and describing developmentally appropriate practice in early childhood programs serving young children. A 1986 statement was expanded and released in book form the next year (see Bredekamp 1986; 1987). The concept of *developmentally appropriate* was certainly not new, having been used by developmental psychologists for more than a century in reference to age-related and individual human variation. NAEYC, however, was motivated by two factors to go on record with more specific guidance for teachers: by the launch of its national program accreditation system, whose standards necessitated clearer interpretation of quality in early childhood practice, and by the growing trend to push down curriculum and teaching methods more appropriate for older children to kindergarten and preschool programs.

A decade later, NAEYC (1996) revisited its position statement on developmentally appropriate practice in response to new knowledge, the changing context, and critiques from within and beyond the profession. Among the major issues reflected in that revised statement and the book containing it (Bredekamp & Copple 1997) were these: the teacher as decision maker; the importance of goals for children being both challenging and achievable; and expanding the basic definition of developmentally appropriate practice to

> We enter and stay in the field because we believe that our work can make a significant difference in the lives of children and their families, and so make a profound and lasting contribution to society.

include consideration of social and cultural context. Later, to more clearly communicate the concepts of the 1996 statement, NAEYC published *Basics of Developmentally Appropriate Practice: An Introduction for Teachers of Children 3 to 6* (Copple & Bredekamp 2006).

The current position statement, on which this book is based, was propelled less by critiques from within the field than by the infusion of new knowledge to guide practice and by the rapidly changing context in which early childhood programs operate—including the growing role of public schools and the increasing focus on narrowing the achievement gap. Further, in 2005 NAEYC significantly revised its Early Childhood Program Standards that identify key components of quality programs. To ensure the consistency of NAEYC's most influential sets of guidelines for practice—the Early Childhood Program Standards and the Position Statement on Developmentally Appropriate Practice—revisiting the position statement was timely.

This series of books builds on the fundamental principles articulated in 1997 and emphasizes several interrelated themes:

Excellence and equity. Achievement gaps—real and present early in life—persist not because children are lacking in any way but because they lack opportunities to learn. Although the current emphasis on accountability and learning gaps has led to inappropriate practices in some classrooms and raised concerns among early childhood educators, the field has long been commited to improving all children's life chances. A prime example, of course, is Head Start. We know that excellent early childhood education can make a difference, and we simply cannot be content with the inequities in early experience that contribute to school failure and lifelong negative consequences for so many of our nation's children.

Intentionality and effectiveness. Good early childhood teachers are purposeful in the decisions they make about their practices, but they also attend to the consequences of those decisions. The current widespread recognition of the value of early education, as well as the explosion in state funding for prekindergarten programs, derives almost exclusively from its effectiveness in producing positive short- and long-term outcomes for children. Holding ourselves accountable for learning and developmental outcomes (as long as they are the right outcomes) is actually evidence of our increased commitment to all children.

Continuity and change. Just as human development through the life span is marked by both continuity and change, so too must be any document that is designed to guide educational practice that reflects knowledge of development. Therefore, the 2009 position statement preserves the enduring values of our

We simply cannot be content with the inequities in early experience that contribute to school failure and lifelong negative consequences for so many of our nation's children.

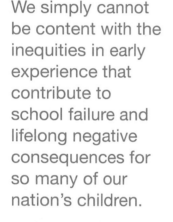

field—commitment to the whole child; recognition of the value of play; respect and responsiveness to individual and cultural diversity; and partnerships with families. At the same time, it has responded to the changing and expanding knowledge base about effective practices in addressing these values as well as improving curriculum, teaching, and assessment. Further, the statement challenges our profession to be more precise and clear when advocating for or criticizing practices, from play to structured curriculum.

Joy and learning. In revisiting the position statement in light of new knowledge and the changing context, we were repeatedly reminded of the core value that cuts across all of our work: Certainly an important and legitimate focus of early care and education is helping children toward becoming productive, responsible adults; but we want their childhood years to be full of joy. High-quality early childhood experiences help equip tomorrow's adults, but childhood is and should be its own special time of life. And it is our responsibility to cultivate children's delight in exploring and understanding their world. Early childhood is and should be a time of laughter, love, play, and great fun. While we still believe that fun for fun's sake is an inadequate rationale for planning a program, we also believe strongly that healthy development and learning cannot occur without attention to children's pleasure and interest.

At the same time, we shouldn't forget how much sheer pleasure children obtain from learning something new, mastering a skill after much effort, or solving a challenging problem. Think of the big smile on a baby's face when she pulls herself up for the first time, a preschooler's pride in writing his own name, the glee that accompanies the first independent bike ride, the look of accomplishment when a first-grader reads "a whole book" for the first time, or the "aha" look on a second-grader's face when she finally understands how to add two-digit numbers quickly. Human beings strive for mastery, and we feel both power and pleasure in our own accomplishments.

We conclude with a reminder (though experienced early childhood practitioners will scarcely need it) about why our field values developmentally appropriate practice in the first place. Seeing children joyfully, physically, and intellectually engaged in meaningful learning about their world and everyone and everything in it is the truest measure of our success as early childhood educators.

It is through developmentally appropriate practice that we create a safe, nurturing, and supportive place for young children to experience those unique joys of childhood.

> It is our responsibility to cultivate children's delight in exploring and understanding their world. Early childhood is and should be a time of laughter, love, play, and great fun.

What Is Developmentally Appropriate Practice?

Key Messages of the Position Statement

The NAEYC position statement on developmentally appropriate practice reflects both continuity and change in the early childhood field. Still central since its last iteration (NAEYC 1996) are our fundamental commitments to **excellence and equity** in educating children and our core understanding of how children learn and develop. At the same time, new knowledge gained over the last two decades has deepened that understanding, allowing us to revise and refine our ideas about how to promote every child's optimal development and learning.

What Is Developmentally Appropriate Practice?

- Developmentally appropriate practice requires both meeting children where they are—which means that teachers must get to know them well—and enabling them to reach goals that are both challenging and achievable.

- All teaching practices should be appropriate to children's age and developmental status, attuned to them as unique individuals, and responsive to the social and cultural contexts in which they live.

- Developmentally appropriate practice does not mean making things easier for children. Rather, it means ensuring that goals and experiences are suited to their learning and development *and* challenging enough to promote their progress and interest.

- Best practice is based on knowledge—not on assumptions—of how children learn and develop. The research base yields major principles in human development and learning (the position statement articulates 12 such principles). Those principles, along with evidence about curriculum and teaching effectiveness, form a solid basis for decision making in early care and education.

 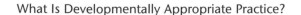

A Call to Reduce the Achievement Gap

- Because in the United States children's learning opportunities often differ sharply with family income and education, ethnicity, and language background, sizable achievement gaps exist between demographic groups. Emerging early in life and persisting throughout the school years, these disparities have serious consequences for children and for society as a whole. Narrowing the gaps must be a priority for early childhood educators as well as policy makers.

- When young children have not had the learning opportunities they require in order to succeed in school, early childhood programs need to provide even more extended, enriched, and intensive learning experiences than they do for children who have had a wealth of such experiences outside of the program or school. The earlier in life those experiences are provided, the better the results for children. Parent engagement strategies, health services, and mental health supports are also critical.

Comprehensive, Effective Curriculum

- All the domains of children's development and learning interrelate. For example, because social factors strongly influence cognitive development and academic competence—and the cognitive domain influences the social domain—teachers must foster learning and development in both, as well as in the emotional and physical domains.

- Effective, developmentally appropriate curriculum is based on what is known about the interrelationships and sequences of ideas, so that children's later abilities and understandings can be built on those already acquired. At the same time, the rate and pattern of each child's learning is unique. An effective teacher must account for all these factors, maintaining high expectations while setting challenging, achievable goals and providing the right amount and type of scaffolding for each child.

- Children's learning experiences across the early childhood years (birth to age 8) need to be far better integrated and aligned, particularly between pre-kindergarten and K–3. Education quality and outcomes would improve substantially if elementary teachers incorporated the best of preschool's emphases and practices (e.g., attention to the whole child; integrated, meaningful learning; parent engagement) and if preschool teachers made more use of those elementary-grade practices that are valuable for younger children, as well (e.g., robust content, attention to learning progressions in curriculum and teaching).

Improving Teaching and Learning

- A teacher's moment-by-moment actions and interactions with children are the most powerful determinant of learning outcomes and development. Curriculum is very important, but what the teacher does is paramount.

- Both child-guided and teacher-guided experiences are vital to children's development and learning. Developmentally appropriate programs provide substantial periods of time when children may select activities to pursue from among the rich choices teachers have prepared.

- Rather than diminishing children's learning by reducing the time devoted to academic activities, play promotes key abilities that enable children to learn successfully. In high-level dramatic play, for example, the collaborative planning of roles and scenarios and the impulse control required to stay within the play's constraints develop children's self-regulation, symbolic thinking, memory, and language—capacities critical to later learning, social competence, and school success.

- Because of how they spend their time outside of school, many young children now lack the ability to play at the high level of complexity and engagement that affords so many cognitive, social, and emotional benefits. As a result, it is vital for early childhood settings to provide opportunities for sustained high-level play and for teachers to actively support children's progress toward such play.

- Effective teachers are intentional in their use of a variety of approaches and strategies to support children's interest and ability in each learning domain. Besides embedding significant learning in play, routines, and interest areas, strong programs also provide carefully planned curriculum that focuses children's attention on a particular concept or topic. Further, skilled teachers adapt curriculum to the group they are teaching and to each individual child to promote optimal learning and development.

- To ensure that teachers are able to provide care and education of high quality, they must be well prepared, participate in ongoing professional development, and receive sufficient support and compensation.

Core Considerations of Developmentally Appropriate Practce

Every day, early childhood practitioners make a great many decisions, both long-term and short-term. As they do so, they need to keep in mind the identified goals for children's learning and development and be intentional in helping children achieve these goals. The core of developmentally appropriate practice lies in this intentionality, in the knowledge that practitioners consider when they are making decisions, and in their always aiming for goals that are both challenging and achievable for children.

- **Knowing about child development and learning.**
  Knowing what is typical at each age and stage of early development is crucial. This knowledge, based on research, helps us decide which experiences are best for children's learning and development.

- **Knowing what is individually appropriate.**
  What we learn about specific children helps us teach and care for each child as an individual. By continually observing children's play and interaction with the physical environment and others, we learn about each child's interests, abilities, and developmental progress.

- **Knowing what is culturally important.**
  We must make an effort to get to know the children's families and learn about the values, expectations, and factors that shape their lives at home and in their communities. This background information helps us provide meaningful, relevant, and respectful learning experiences for each child and family.

Principles of Child Development and Learning

Developmentally appropriate practice is informed by what we know from theory and literature about how children develop and learn. In particular, a review of that literature yields a number of well supported generalizations, or principles.

No linear listing of principles—including the one below, excerpted from NAEYC's position statement on developmentally appropriate practice—can do justice to the complexity of the phenomenon that is child development and learning. While the list is comprehensive, it certainly is not all-inclusive. Each principle describes an individually contributing factor; but just as all domains of development and learning are interrelated, so too do the principles interconnect. For example, the influence of cultural differences and individual differences, each highlighted in a separate principle below, cuts across all the other principles. That is, the implication of any principle often differs as a function of cultural or individual givens.

A complete discussion of the knowledge base that informs developmentally appropriate practice is clearly beyond the scope of this chapter. Each of the principles rests on an extensive research base.

All the limitations of such a list notwithstanding, collectively the principles that follow form a solid basis for decision making—for decisions at all levels about how best to meet the needs of young children in general, and for decisions by teachers, programs, and families about the strengths and needs of individual children, with all their variations in prior experiences, abilities and talents, home language and English proficiency, personalities and temperaments, and community and cultural backgrounds.

1. All the domains of development and learning—physical, social and emotional, and cognitive—are important, and they are closely interrelated. Children's development and learning in one domain influence and are influenced by what takes place in other domains.

2. Many aspects of children's learning and development follow well documented sequences, with later abilities, skills, and knowledge building on those already acquired.

3. Development and learning proceed at varying rates from child to child, as well as at uneven rates across different areas of a child's individual functioning.

4. Development and learning result from a dynamic and continuous interaction of biological maturation and experience.

5. Early experiences have profound effects, both cumulative and delayed, on a child's development and learning; and optimal periods exist for certain types of development and learning to occur.

6. Development proceeds toward greater complexity, self-regulation, and symbolic or representational capacities.

7. Children develop best when they have secure, consistent relationships with responsive adults and opportunities for positive relationships with peers.

8. Development and learning occur in and are influenced by multiple social and cultural contexts.

9. Always mentally active in seeking to understand the world around them, children learn in a variety of ways; a wide range of teaching strategies and interactions is effective in supporting all these kinds of learning.

10. Play is an important vehicle for developing self-regulation as well as for promoting language, cognition, and social competence.

11. Development and learning advance when children are challenged to achieve at a level just beyond their current mastery, and also when they have many opportunities to practice newly acquired skills.

12. Children's experiences shape their motivation and approaches to learning, such as persistence, initiative, and flexibility; in turn, these dispositions and behaviors affect their learning and development.

For more information about developmentally appropriate practice, the Core Considerations, and the Principles of Child Development and Learning, scan this QR code or go to www.naeyc.org/position statements/dap to read the NAEYC position statement "Developmentally Appropriate Practice in Early Childhood Programs Serving Children From Birth Through Age 8," adopted in 2009.

To Be an Excellent Teacher

Carol Copple and Sue Bredekamp

Developmentally appropriate practice is at the core of being an excellent early childhood professional—that is the central premise of this book.

Developmentally appropriate practice is grounded in the research on child development and learning and in the knowledge base regarding educational effectiveness. From this knowledge base, we know a great deal about how children develop and learn at various ages and what approaches and conditions tend to work best for them.

This knowledge is the starting place for teachers in the many decisions they make—the long-term ones as well as the minute-by-minute ones: how to organize the environment to help children do their best, how to plan curriculum that engages children and helps them reach important goals, how to adapt teaching strategies for the group and for individual children—the list goes on and on. But to the question "Is this decision developmentally appropriate?" the response always begins with two words: "It depends." That is, whether a given teaching practice or policy is developmentally appropriate depends: for which child or children? . . . for which families? . . . in what context? . . . for what purpose?

This chapter describes what excellent teachers decide to do in their classrooms to translate the developmentally appropriate practice framework, outlined in the position statement, into high-quality experiences for children, birth to age 8.

To be an excellent teacher means . . .

being intentional

Whenever you see a great classroom, one in which children are learning and thriving, you can be sure that the teachers (and the administrators who support them) are highly intentional. In everything that good teachers do—

creating the environment, considering the curriculum and tailoring it to the children as individuals, planning learning experiences, and interacting with children and families—they are purposeful and thoughtful. As they make myriad decisions, big and small, they keep in mind the outcomes they seek. Even in responding to unexpected opportunities—"teachable moments"—intentional teachers are guided by the outcomes the program is trying to help children reach and by their knowledge of child development and learning.

Having a clear sense of how all aspects of the program relate to and promote the desired goals contributes to an intentional teacher's effectiveness. Learning goals are usually identified for groups of children within a given age span. But teachers must determine where each child is in relation to a goal and adjust their teaching accordingly. For example, some children who live in poverty are behind what is typical for other children in their age group in such areas as vocabulary, math and literacy learning, and self-regulation. For these children, excellent teachers, schools, and programs provide more extended, enriched, and intensive learning opportunities—such as more small-group activities and one-on-one interaction—to accelerate their learning and help them to catch up.

Similarly, in serving children with disabilities and other special needs, teachers' attention to individual variation is essential. In addition to age-appropriate goals, an individualized plan for such a child will identify individually appropriate goals, which teachers implement in conjunction with families and specialists. In many cases, the plan necessitates more systematic, intentional teaching for the child to function and learn well in an inclusive setting.

Having their objectives and plans in mind, intentional teachers are well prepared to tell others—parents, administrators, colleagues—about what they

This chapter was first published in *Developmentally Appropriate Practice in Early Childhood Programs Serving Children From Birth Through Age 8* (Copple & Bredekamp 2009).

are doing. Not only do they know what to do, they also know *why* they are doing it and can describe their purposes.

Excellence in All Areas of Practice

Excellent teachers are intentional in *all* aspects of their role. The position statement identifies these areas as: creating a caring community of learners, teaching to enhance development and learning, planning curriculum to achieve important goals, assessing children's development and learning, and establishing reciprocal relationships with families.

The various facets of the teacher's role are blended into a whole, which is illustrated here as a five-pointed star. Each point of the star represents one vital part of what teachers and early childhood programs must do to promote children's learning and development and enable them to reach important goals. Clearly, these five facets are closely interrelated, and none can be left out or shortchanged without seriously weakening the whole.

To be an excellent teacher means . . .
creating a caring community of learners

Children learn and develop best when they are part of a community of learners—a community in which all participants consider and contribute to one another's well-being and learning. To create such a classroom community, good teachers make a point of getting to know every child and family well. They make the effort to learn about each child's personality, abilities, interests, and ways of learning, and they work to build a strong sense of group identity among the children in the group.

Toward this end, teachers plan ways for children to work and play together collaboratively, and they work to bring each child's home culture and language into the shared culture of the class. They make a point of including children with special needs in all aspects of the program, so that not only do these children benefit but *all* the children in the group gain an understanding of how all people are similar and different. Inclusion of children with disabilities and other special needs means more than their simply being present in the classroom; it means, rather, they are active participants as part of the classroom community.

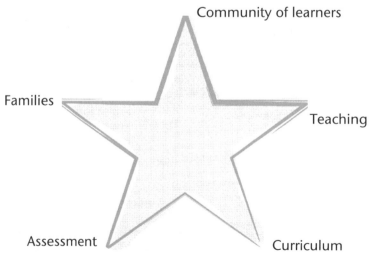

The excellent teacher makes it a priority to develop a warm, positive relationship with each child. This relationship is vital to young children's learning and development in all areas, and it makes effective, positive guidance possible. In the early childhood years, guidance should not be just something teachers do so they can get on with the curriculum. Instead, children's self-regulation and social and emotional competence are essential curricular goals in their own right. These capabilities do in fact help children to learn and succeed in school (Hyson 2008; McClelland, Acock, & Morrison 2006). Equally important, they have great intrinsic value for children's present and future lives.

Guidance is effective when teachers help children learn how to make better decisions the next time. Excellent early childhood teachers recognize children's conflicts and "misbehavior" as learning opportunities. Hence, they listen carefully to what children say, model problem solving, and give patient reminders of rules (and reasons for them)—this, too, is effective guidance. A caring community of learners provides young children with a foundation that they will carry with them into their future lives in and out of school.

To be an excellent teacher means . . .

teaching to enhance development and learning

Good teachers continually use their knowledge and judgment to make intentional decisions about which materials, interactions, and learning experiences are likely to be most effective for the group and for each individual child in it. Many different teaching approaches and strategies have value in the early childhood classroom.

Excellent Teachers Use a Wide Range of Teaching Strategies

An effective teacher makes use of the strategy that fits a particular situation and the purpose or purposes she has in mind. She considers what the child or children already know and can do and the learning goals for the specific situation. Often she may try one strategy, see that it doesn't work, and then try something else. She has a variety of strategies at the ready and remains flexible and observant so that she can determine which to use. Here are some of the strategies excellent teachers have at their disposal:

- Teachers **acknowledge** what children do or say. They let children know that they have noticed by giving children positive attention, sometimes through comments, sometimes through just sitting nearby and observing (*Thanks for your help, Kavi*).

- Teachers **encourage** persistence and effort rather than just praising and evaluating what the child has done (*You tried many times to reach that block!*).

- Teachers **give specific feedback** rather than general comments (*Oops, almost! The beanbag didn't land in the hoop again! How about if you stand a little closer to the hoop next time?*).

- Teachers **model** attitudes, ways of approaching problems, and behavior toward others, showing children rather than just telling them (*Hmm, that didn't work. I wonder why? Can you help me try this again? Thank you!*).

10

- Teachers **demonstrate** when they show the correct way to do something. This usually applies to a procedure that needs to be done in a certain way (*See how hard I rub my hands together to wash them? Look at all the soap bubbles! All over my hands!*).

- Teachers **create or add challenge** so that a task goes a bit beyond what the children can already do. For example, when the caregiver asks a toddler to complete a one-step task (*Place the blocks in this basket*), he may add difficulty by adding another step (*Place the blocks in this basket, then put the basket here on the shelf*). In other cases, teachers **reduce challenge** to meet children where they are (*Hand me a block, please*).

- Teachers **ask questions** that provoke children's thinking (*What made that sound?*).

- Teachers **give assistance** (e.g., a cue or hint) to help children work on the edge of their current competence (*What color is* this *ball? Look! It's the same color as Clifford the Dog, right over there*).

- Teachers **provide information**, directly giving children facts, verbal labels, and other information (*This one with a tail is called a mouse*).

- Teachers **give directions** for children's action or behavior (*Please put all the red blocks in this basket*).

Note: Throughout this book, the term *caregiver* is always intended to refer to any adult responsible for the direct care and education of infants and toddlers in a group setting.

Some of these strategies involve less action and direction on the part of the adult and more on the part of the child; in others, the adult is more proactive or directive. Both kinds of strategies may be used in any context.

Although play is inherently an open-ended and child-guided activity, the teacher may directly provide information, create challenges, supply vocabulary, and otherwise enhance what children gain in the play setting.

All these strategies are also effective in teaching children with disabilities and other special needs. However, teachers may use more systematic instruction to help children acquire a skill or change an unacceptable behavior. For example, when working with children with challenging behaviors, an effective strategy is for teachers to identify the conditions that tend to propel the behavior and the consequences that usually follow. Then, teachers can anticipate and work to prevent problem behavior, as well as make sure that the negative behavior does not achieve its goal—as when hitting makes another child give up a toy. At the same time, teachers can "catch them doing something right," giving such children positive attention and encouragement for desired behaviors when they occur.

Excellent Teachers Scaffold Children's Learning

Developmentally appropriate goals are *both* challenging *and* achievable. The most effective learning experiences build on what children already know and can do, but also encourage them to stretch a reasonable amount toward a new level of achievement.

Of course, learners cannot spend all their time "on their tiptoes." They also need plenty of opportunity to practice the skills they have just begun

acquiring. They need to feel solid mastery and a sense of being successful, of the goal having been achieved, rather than always feeling rushed on to the next challenge. Young children will often practice newly acquired or developing skills during their play, as when a toddler repeatedly fills and dumps a bucket of toys. Once children have mastered a new skill or concept, they are ready for the next stretch.

As a child begins a new challenge, he may need some support from the teacher to enable him to manage it. A skilled teacher doesn't overdo the help. The aim is to provide the least amount of support that the child needs to do something he cannot quite do on his own. For example, if the goal is to take a few steps without holding onto the teacher's hand, the teacher might stand beside the child as he walks, so that he can grab the adult's hand as needed to keep from falling. If, instead, the teacher held the boy's hand throughout, whether he was unsteady or not, he would be less likely to learn to balance on his own.

As the child begins to acquire the new skill or understanding, the teacher gradually reduces her support. Soon the child who has been receiving assistance will be able to handle the skill or task independently. Because the teacher provides support only as long as it is needed, what she does is called *scaffolding*—like the platforms painters stand on to reach spots high up on a house they couldn't otherwise reach and then take away when the job is done. For example, for a toddler who is usually rejected by the other children, a teacher may at first directly coach her in how to successfully enter play (*Try saying, "I would like to play"*). If the child's overtures are successful, her new behavior is encouraged by the other children's responses, and the teacher can withdraw.

Excellent teachers use scaffolding to help children progress in all areas of learning and development throughout the day. And their scaffolding can take many forms. They might ask a question, point out a discrepancy, give a hint about an aspect of the problem or task that the child has missed, add a cue or support such as a picture or diagram, take the child's hand, or pair the child with a peer so that the two can be successful with their combined strengths.

To be an excellent teacher means . . .
planning curriculum to achieve important goals

The curriculum consists of the knowledge and skills to be acquired in the educational program as well as the plans for experiences through which children's learning will take place. Research clearly demonstrates that children learn more in programs where there is a well planned and implemented curriculum (Bowman, Donovan, & Burns 2000; Landry 2008; Schweinhart & Weikart 1997). Thus, it is essential for every early childhood setting—be it a school, a center, or a family child care home—to have a high-quality curriculum in written form and for teachers and care providers to use it to guide their planning and implementation of learning experiences. And it is equally essential for them to adapt their plans and the actual learning experiences to help individual children make progress toward the curriculum's goals. To be effective, a curriculum must have goals that are clearly defined, shared, and understood by all stakeholders, including administrators, teachers, and families (NAEYC & NAECS/SDE 2003). Then the curriculum must be designed to address these goals in a unified, coherent way.

A central question informs the development of curriculum: What goals do we have for the children during the time that they are with us? In other words, what significant learning and development outcomes do we want to see children attain? A growing research base is helping to identify certain skills, abilities, knowledge, and approaches to learning that enable children to succeed in school and beyond. This knowledge base has informed the work of states, professional organizations, and other entities in creating standards for what children should know and be able to do. High-quality, developmentally appropriate standards are important guides in curriculum development and in teaching. In cases where standards are not developmentally appropriate and need to be substantially improved, it is important for teachers, parents, and administrators to work together to change them.

A curriculum is much more than a collection of activities. It provides the framework for developing a coherent set of learning experiences that enables children to reach the identified goals. Whether the curriculum is a published product or one written by teachers, it must be effective and comprehensive in addressing all the developmental domains and important content areas. Excellent teachers continually refer to the curriculum to give coherence to the classroom experiences they plan. Teachers must be familiar with the learning goals that comprise the curriculum and carefully shape its learning experiences to enable each child to gain those understandings, knowledge, and skills.

Sequence matters in curriculum. In many areas of development and learning, some concepts and skills logically come first and others build on them (e.g., the understanding of the alphabetic principle lays the foundation for reading). And in some instances, it appears that what a child most readily learns first and what comes later depend on brain organization and the sequence of brain development. For example, phonological awareness proceeds from the child noticing gross auditory differences (e.g., the separations between words and between syllables), to noticing distinctions that are more refined (e.g., individual phonemes) (Lonigan 2006). Knowledge of such progressions guides the excellent teacher in planning the sequence of experiences and materials—for the group and for individual children. Further, this knowledge enables the teacher to scaffold children in taking the logical next steps in their individual developmental progression.

Meaningful connections are another priority in the curriculum planning of good teachers. Young children learn best when the concepts, vocabulary, and skills they encounter are related to something they already know and care about and when the new learnings are themselves interconnected in meaningful, coherent ways. Children do not learn as readily when information and experiences are presented in isolated, unrelated chunks.

For their part, excellent teachers make every effort—adapting the curriculum if necessary—to allow children to have sustained learning time for a given topic or skill. When learning is meaningful, integrated, and in-depth, it is more likely to be engaging. It is also more likely to stick.

To be an excellent teacher means . . .
assessing children's development and learning

If curriculum is the path children and their teachers take toward the desired goals, assessment is the process of looking at children's progress toward those goals. Thoughtful attention to assessment is essential to developmentally appropriate practice in order to

• Monitor children's development and learning

• Guide planning and decision making

• Identify children who might benefit from special services or supports

• Report and communicate with others, including families (McAfee, Leong, & Bodrova 2004)

Assessing children by observing and talking with them and closely considering their work is key for teachers in their efforts to get to know each child and his or her abilities and needs. Getting valid information about young children is made more challenging by several realities: They grow and change rapidly, their development is uneven, and they are easily distracted. One guideline is to never rely on a single assessment measure. Potentially useful sources of information are observation, examination of each child's work, talking with a child in a "clinical interview" format (an extended dialogue in which the adult seeks to discern the child's concepts or strategies), individually administered assessments, and talking with families. Information about children also should be gathered in different settings or contexts.

Finally, assessing children in developmentally appropriate ways requires attention to what is

• **Appropriate for the child's age or developmental status**—anticipating and responding to the age/developmental characteristics of children that are likely to influence the validity of assessment methods

- **Individually appropriate**—including making choices and adaptations of assessment methods to get the best information about a particular child

- **Culturally appropriate**—considering what will make sense to a child given his or her linguistic and cultural background (e.g., avoiding materials that will not be understood), as well as interpreting a child's behavior in light of the social and cultural contexts in which the child lives (e.g., not taking a limited verbal response to the test situation to mean she is deficient in language or intellect)

Assessment information is vital to guide teachers' planning. The excellent teacher uses her observations and other information gathered to inform her planning and teaching, giving careful consideration to the learning experiences needed by the group as a whole and by each individual child. By observing what children explore, what draws their interest, and what they say and do, the teacher determines how to adapt the environment, materials, or daily routines. The teacher can make an activity simpler or more complex according to what individual children are ready for. Then, her follow-up plans can include giving children repeated experiences with an idea or skill to get a solid grasp of it. Effective planning also means considering where the child or group of children might go next.

To be an excellent teacher means . . .

establishing reciprocal relationships with families

Parents are the most important people in their child's life. They know their child well, and their preferences and choices matter. Excellent teachers work hard to develop reciprocal relationships with families, with communication and respect in both directions.

The effective teacher recognizes that families are an invaluable source of information about their child as an individual, and she understands that a family wants to know that their knowledge and insights are regarded as important. Besides, by drawing on each family's in-depth knowledge of their child, she also can learn about their home and community environment, including its cultural dimensions. This context is critical in making classroom decisions that are appropriate for each child, as well as in fostering positive relationships with the parents themselves.

For their part, early childhood professionals have a lot to share with families. They have valuable knowledge of and experience with children in general. And teachers can give parents the particulars about what their own child said and did that day: what he is exploring, learning, and achieving in the class. Teacher–parent communication is important in achieving a degree of consistency in the ways that the significant adults in the child's life guide and relate to that child. And young children feel more secure when they see that the adults who care about them share trust and respect.

When it comes to making decisions about a child, sharing that decision making with families is important. Teachers and families are a partnership, working for the best interests of the child. Good teachers take intentional steps to build such partnerships, including

- Making family members feel welcome in the classroom and inviting their participation in the program

- Working to create a relationship that allows for open dialogue

- Maintaining frequent, positive, two-way communication (planned conferences and messages sent home are important, as is day-to-day communication with families)

- Acknowledging parents' choices and goals for their child and responding with sensitivity and respect to their preferences and concerns

In our diverse society, teachers need to be tuned into the cultural dimension in their relationships with families (see "Bridging Cultural Differences" on the next page). Excellent teachers know that listening well and keeping an open mind about different perspectives are vital where cultural differences exist and essential with *all* the families they serve.

Seeing the Bigger Picture

The primary purpose of this chapter was to answer seemingly simple questions: What is developmentally appropriate practice? What does it look like in the classroom? On one level the answers, too, are simple: It is practice that promotes young children's optimal learning and development. It is what excellent teachers do in the classroom. But on another level, the answers are highly complex, as this chapter has tried to make clear: Enacting the concept of developmentally appropriate practice in a classroom is complex because the answer to "How do I know if a given practice is developmentally appropriate?" always begins with "It depends."

Given that complexity, it is maybe no wonder that despite NAEYC's decades-long advocacy of such practice, what is and is not developmentally appropriate is still subject to misinterpretation, misconceptions, and misrepresentation. For example, some of the most persistent myths are

- "Direct instruction is always inappropriate"

- "Developmentally appropriate practice is maturationist" (i.e., teachers are encouraged to simply wait for children's development to unfold rather than actively promoting it)

- "Developmentally appropriate practice is soft" (i.e., teachers are urged to put off introduction of robust subject content until later grades)

Focus on Infants and Toddlers

Bridging Cultural Differences

Sometimes a family expresses a strong preference or acts in a way that you feel conflicts with what's best for the child and consistent with developmentally appropriate practice. When this happens, you should take the opportunity to find out more about the other person's perspective. The preliminary conversation may bring to light some cultural differences, and you may feel out of your depth. But also know that the family may feel lost or confused by the differences in how *you* view children. What you need to keep in mind when you encounter cultural differences is this: When a family behavior or preference seems to be at odds with developmentally appropriate practice, do not jump to negative judgments.

Here's a true story that illustrates the point:

> Jamal's father and mother insisted that he not go outside to play. The teacher, Ms. Harrison, wanted to insist right back that *all* the children, including Jamal, were going outside to play. But when she engaged the parents in a dialogue about their reasons, she found out that their concern was Jamal getting sand in his hair, which they found unacceptable. Together the family and teachers reached a solution: All the children would be required to wear shower caps during sand play, just as they wore smocks for painting and water play.

Culture is deeply rooted and highly complex, and teachers cannot have a detailed understanding of every culture they encounter through the children and families they serve. More importantly, teachers cannot know how different cultures and expectations will interact, or what form the cultural norms take for each individual or family.

Hitting a cultural bump means you first need to learn more about the family and their culture. You can do this by observing the family members interacting with their children. You can listen to their expectations for their child's behavior and interaction with adults and peers and try to come to an understanding of the family's beliefs about children and childrearing. Then, take some time to comment (with no judgment implied) on what you see, and talk to the family about your concept of child development as well as the teaching and care practices used in the program.

Families will want to know that what their children will learn in the early childhood program is in harmony with their values. Aiming for harmony between program and home can come about through *culturally responsive* practices. Cultural responsiveness can be compared to music, where notes that are harmonious aren't the exact same notes, but they do go together. The point is to avoid driving a wedge between children and their families by continuing with practices that aren't mutually agreeable.

To create harmony even in the face of differing practices, it is important to move away from viewing contrasting practices as right or wrong, instead thinking of them simply as different. This change in perspective doesn't mean that "anything goes." Nor does the change mean that you should abandon your commitment to good practice. Remember, just because it's *cultural* doesn't always mean it's good for children. First, you must seek to understand the family's perspective and the identity issues involved, and then you can better judge what's actually harmful or beneficial for the particular child. Obviously, even while being open to accepting cultural differences as valid and right, you must consider the nonnegotiable legal and ethical boundaries involved in caring for children.

So when your professional knowledge about what children need is in contrast with the practice of a particular family or individual, the solution lies in *communicating about the differences.* Together everyone involved can figure out what to do about those differences, as Jamal's family and teacher did with their shower cap solution. Professional knowledge is valuable, but there is always room to expand on it. The goal, unless a family sees it differently, is to keep children safe, trusting, developing, growing, *and* connected to their culture *while also* learning how to operate in the world outside it.

Janet Gonzalez-Mena is an early childhood consultant who writes frequently on issues of culture in early care and education

To challenge these and other myths—and also to communicate more clearly among ourselves and with others—the early childhood field needs to widen the lens through which we view practice, as well as become more precise in how we describe best practice.

The metaphor of a lens here is useful in two ways. First, a camera lens has the capacity to narrow as well as widen the view we see. It can be turned on one individual or expanded to include a whole group. For example, consider how different the picture looks when we focus on a child only as an individual, as opposed to widening the lens to include the child's peers or family members. Second, a lens can be brought into sharper focus for greater clarification and precision, as the following example illustrates.

Consider the critically important role of *play* in young children's development. Sometimes early childhood advocates make the sweeping assertion that "children learn through play." There is truth in the statement, but it needs qualification. There are many different kinds of play—constructive play, pretend play, games, rough-and-tumble play—offering different potential benefits for children. For instance, mature dramatic play (e.g., developing a play scenario and staying within its constraints) contributes significantly to children's self-regulation, while simply manipulating play objects in the dramatic play area (e.g., putting a dish in the play oven, taking it out) does not promote self-regulation skills.

And evidence suggests that higher-level play does not automatically unfold on its own (Hirsh-Pasek et al. 2009). Teachers have essential roles in ensuring that play meets its potential for children. Thus, to effectively use play to promote children's development and learning, we must sharpen the lens through which we view play. And as we advocate for play and other practices we think serve children best, it is particularly vital that we be clear in our own thinking and precise in our communication with parents, administrators, and policy makers.

Returning to the lens metaphor, there's another way that adjusting our lens to view a wider frame helps us think about practice in more useful ways. It is what is known as *both/and* thinking. While polarized ways of thinking ("The best way must be *either* this *or* that") are prevalent in debates about education, a more productive route is to recognize that developmentally appropriate practice often means using a mix of approaches or modifying one approach depending on the situation.

For example, the question "Do children learn best when the teacher dictates the course of the activity or when children do?" sets up a false choice. Evidence indicates that *both* child-guided *and* teacher-guided experiences play important roles in children's learning and development (Epstein 2007).

Finally, here are a few very important *both/ands* to keep in mind.

Excellent teachers know . . .
it's *both* what you teach *and* how you teach

The early childhood field has paid a great deal of attention to pedagogy—the *how* of teaching and learning—and has identified characteristics of effectiveness that have held up over time, such as meaningful, active learning and individualizing our teaching methods to the learner. Certainly the importance of worthwhile content has been noted (e.g., Katz & Chard 2000); but on the whole, content (the *what* of learning) has been given less emphasis in early education than have the processes of teaching and learning. Research and student achievement data (especially for the primary grades and beyond), along with common sense, indicate that what we teach and how we teach it both matter in educating young children.

Sometimes research does not yet provide clear answers about the best teaching methods and the most important learning goals at a given age or grade level. But when such answers exist, early childhood teachers need this knowledge and the professional development and support to enable them to understand and use it in their classrooms.

Excellent teachers know . . .
it's *both* teacher-guided *and* child-guided experiences

Whether in child-guided experience or in teacher-guided instruction, the most significant educational experiences are those that deeply engage children's minds. There are classrooms in which children are free to choose and play but that offer them little sustained involvement in activities and play situations. Others hum with children's interest and involvement in their activities. Likewise, children can be highly engaged in a well-planned and lively adult-guided experience. Or they may be bored, frustrated, or overwhelmed in an inappropriate one.

Both/And Thinking in Early Childhood Practice

One of the most well received and oft-quoted sections of NAEYC's 1996 position statement on developmentally appropriate practice was its challenge to the field to move from *either/or* to *both/and* thinking. The call was in response to a recurring tendency in the American discourse on education: the polarizing into *either/or* choices on many questions that were more fruitfully seen as *both/ands*.

Some of that polarizing continues today. For example, regardless of the subject area, heated debates continue about whether children benefit more from *either* direct instruction *or* child-guided activity. In reality, each approach works best for different kinds of learning, and elements of both can be combined effectively. In studying science, for example, the teacher in one kindergarten classroom may give a 20-minute lecture, while in another classroom children might be given materials and left to explore entirely on their own—neither approach is likely to be effective by itself. A more effective course would be to draw on *both* approaches, with children conducting hands-on experiments guided by teachers who provide clear explanations of concepts and introduce scientific language.

In the process of updating the position statement, it became evident that many in the early childhood field have moved toward valuing the *both/and* way of thinking. However, a new worry arises: that sometimes *both/and* thinking may be applied quite superficially as just a "pinch of this and a dash of that." Most questions about what is and is not developmentally appropriate practice require more nuanced and evidence-based responses.

The following statements are offered as a few examples of the many ways that early childhood practice draws on *both/and* thinking and conveys some of the complexity and interrelationship among the principles that guide our practice.

- Teachers *both* need to have high expectations for all children's learning *and* need to recognize that some children require additional assistance and resources to meet those expectations.

- Children *both* construct their own understanding of concepts *and* benefit from instruction by more competent peers and adults.

- Children benefit *both* from engaging in self-initiated, spontaneous play *and* from teacher-planned and -structured activities, projects, and experiences.

- Children benefit *both* from opportunities to see connections across disciplines through integration of curriculum *and* from opportunities to engage in focused, in-depth study in a content area.

- Children benefit *both* from predictable structure and orderly routine in the learning environment *and* from the teacher's flexibility and responsiveness to children's emerging ideas, needs, and interests.

- Children benefit *both* from opportunities to make meaningful choices *and* from having a clear understanding of the boundaries within which choices are permissible.

- Children benefit *both* from situations that challenge them to work at the edge of their developing capacities *and* from ample opportunities to practice newly acquired skills.

- Children benefit *both* from opportunities to collaborate with peers and acquire a sense of being part of a community *and* from being treated as individuals with their own strengths, interests, and needs.

- Children need to develop *both* a positive sense of their own self-identity *and* respect for other people whose perspectives and experiences may be different from their own.

- Children *both* have enormous capacities to learn and almost boundless curiosity about the world *and* have recognized, age-related limits on their cognitive and linguistic capacities.

- Children who are dual language learners *both* need to acquire proficiency in English *and* need to maintain and further develop their home language.

- Teachers must commit themselves *both* to closing the achievement gap that exists between children of various socioeconomic, cultural, and linguistic groups *and* to viewing every child as capable of achieving.

Excellent teachers know . . .

it's *both* joy *and* learning

Joy and learning are not only both important—they go hand in hand. From infancy, children explore visually, manipulate objects, and experience what Piaget called "pleasure at being a cause" (1962, 91). They love to make things happen. When a baby kicks an object accidentally and hears a noise, she kicks her legs again to try to repeat the effect. Is this pleasure or learning? It's both.

Brain experts testify to the close link of learning and delight:

> A wonderful cycle of learning is driven by the pleasure in play. A child is curious; she explores and discovers. The discovery brings pleasure; the pleasure leads to repetition and practice. Practice brings mastery; mastery brings the pleasure and confidence to once again act on curiosity. All learning—emotional, social, motor and cognitive—is accelerated and facilitated by repetition fueled by the pleasure of play. (Perry, Hogan, & Marlin 2000)

Children love to find out more about their world, seek and master new challenges, and gain in competence (Hyson 2008). Teachers are always more effective when they tap into this natural love of learning rather than dividing work and enjoyment. As some early childhood educators like to put it, children love nothing better than "hard fun."

❖　　　❖　　　❖

This chapter has focused on the kinds of decisions that excellent teachers make that add up to developmentally appropriate practice. Good decisions are never made in a vacuum—some choices are better than others. An excellent teacher's decisions are informed first by what the early childhood field knows about how best to promote children's development and learning. The following chapters focus on infants and toddlers, and describe in a broad way what children's development and learning are like between birth and age 3, along with some major implications of those developmental considerations for practice.

Understanding Development of Infants and Toddlers

Mary Benson McMullen

Babies. Captivating, wondrous, and beguiling. They come into the world fully equipped to enchant us, to draw us in. They challenge us to discover what is most human within ourselves and to act upon these feelings, joyfully and unabashedly to care for, love, and nurture them. Being able to share

with families the journey their children take over the first three years of life, being with those infants and toddlers as they learn, explore, grow, and develop, is a marvelous gift and a tremendous responsibility. Families entrust the physical and psychological health and well-being of their young children to us. They place *in our hands* the care of the developing minds, bodies, and spirits of their youngest family members. (See "In Our Hands," p. 24.) We need to be fully prepared for this role, to be armed with the knowledge and skills to support the day-to-day needs and well-being of children from birth to age 3, while

at the same time providing them with what they need to be successful when they leave our groups.

In this chapter, we look at child development from birth to age 3 broadly, in terms of how we can observe and support it through developmentally appropriate, family-centered, and culturally responsive practices in group settings. This chapter's focus is on development of infants and toddlers without chronic medical conditions or disabilities, not on development that might be impacted by chronic medical conditions or disabilities.

No single chapter can provide all that is important to know about development, but it will provide caregivers a look at accomplishments they will likely observe in the context of group care. The figure below shows the framework for the material in this chapter and a model for optimizing young children's overall health, well-being, and development in groups.

Understanding Infants and Toddlers

Young children follow their own unique timetables for development, with the greatest variance seen during the first three years. Three years seems like a short time to an adult, but the rate of growth and development that occurs from birth to 3 is so rapid, it is useful to break this period down. Rather than dividing it by age, when considering development it is more useful to organize by developmental needs, ways of processing information, and ways of interacting with the environment (Lally & Mangione 2008).

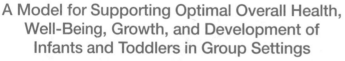

A Model for Supporting Optimal Overall Health, Well-Being, Growth, and Development of Infants and Toddlers in Group Settings

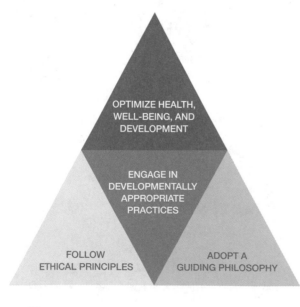

OPTIMIZE HEALTH, WELL-BEING, AND DEVELOPMENT

ENGAGE IN DEVELOPMENTALLY APPROPRIATE PRACTICES

FOLLOW ETHICAL PRINCIPLES

ADOPT A GUIDING PHILOSOPHY

The result is the three ages for birth to 3 presented in the table "Developmental Charateristics of Infants and Toddlers," helping us to characterize young infants, mobile infants, and toddlers. Having distinct categories and understanding the unique developmental needs within each provides information for observations, developmental assessment, and planning, and for making decisions about materials, equipment, and furnishings, as well as considering carefully how to organize groups of children.

Knowledge of Child Development

Knowing child development is fundamental to being a good observer, a critical skill in the continuous assessment and documentation of infants and toddlers (Elicker & McMullen 2013). Careful

Developmental Characteristics of Infants and Toddlers

Period of Birth to 3	Approximate Age	Primary Focus of Development
Young Infants	**Birth to About 9 Months**	**Seeking Security and Sense of Trust**
Young infants need to feel secure and see the world as a trustworthy place—when I am hungry, someone feeds me; when I am sad, lonely, or scared, someone comforts me; when I am wet and uncomfortable, someone responds; and those who take care of me do this with love and tenderness. To build a storehouse of trust, young infants' needs must be met predictably, promptly, and by sensitively responsive practitioners who know them well.		
Mobile Infants	**From 8 Months to About 18 Months**	**Engaging in Multisensory Exploration**
A new stage of life emerges as infants become mobile, rolling, crawling, or toddling through the environment. Much of the mobile infant's day is spent practicing and refining the use of muscles, both large and small, as they grasp, bang, hit, clap, slap, throw, drop, carry, push, and climb around all available surfaces. Mobile infants immerse themselves in independent play and exploration, usually content on their own without engagement from adults or peers. They use everything at their disposal to make meaning of the world, constructing knowledge and building concepts through multisensory exploration.		
Toddlers	**From 16 Months to About 36 Months**	**Defining Identity and Sense of Belonging**
During their second year, mobile infants begin displaying characteristic changes that signal a shift in development. Toddlers actively assert themselves—their sense of self—expressing strong opinions, preferences, desires, and needs. At the same time they also become more socially aware and capable of caring for and about those around them. Toddlers develop a sense of belonging to their group in care, showing preferences for particular peers, and are well aware of their family members.		

observation and ongoing assessment, paired with knowledge from families, contributes to deep knowledge and allows caregivers to individualize care. Observing development informs caregivers about skills and abilities already mastered and now being practiced and consolidated, and helps them plan new experiences that encompass the next developmental steps and challenges.

Philosophy and Principles Supporting Development

Environments that are best at supporting children's healthy growth and optimizing developmental outcomes work under a coherent and ethical guiding philosophy, one supported by all adults in the setting. Developmentally appropriate practice is a guiding philosophy that helps many early childhood education professionals think about, or conceptualize, their practice. The philosophy serves as the foundation for building principles of practice, which are used when making decisions about all interactions and practices. "Guiding Principles of Practice" on page 26 describes seven such principles specific to birth to 3, which we discuss briefly below.

Understand who infants and toddlers are in the context of multiple influences. Recognize that each area of development impacts and is impacted by all others, and that similarly, development occurs in interaction with sociocultural and environmental factors. Thus, young children must be observed and assessed holistically.

Mary Benson McMullen, PhD, is professor of early childhood education at Indiana University in Bloomington. Her current research focuses on fostering physical and psychological well-being through relationship-based practices in children birth to age 3.

Guiding Principles of Practice

Birth-to-3 professionals guided by developmentally appropriate practice

- Understand who infants and toddlers are in the context of multiple influences
- Honor and support *all* children and their families
- Partner fully with families in caring for their children
- Engage in culturally responsive care
- Respect the rights of children
- Invest in caring and supportive relationships throughout the setting
- Respond promptly and sensitively to children's communications

Honor and support *all* young children and their families. Be ready and welcoming of each and every child who walks, crawls, or is carried into the group setting, along with their families, regardless of their beliefs, circumstances, needs, languages, and communication styles. Thus, children and families should find the caregiving environment to be supportive and nonjudgmental.

Partner fully with families in caring for their children. Engage in family-centered practices by respecting families as partners, not clients or customers, and recognize their expertise by honoring the decisions they make about their infants and toddlers (Keyser 2006; Pianta et al. 2012). Thus, families should feel empowered and their capacity to support their child's development bolstered.

Engage in culturally responsive care. Be mindful of all messages conveyed to children and families, verbally and nonverbally, about what is right or wrong, normal or not, and good or bad—all of which contribute to a child's understanding of self as a person worthy of love and of her family as worthy of acceptance. Thus, it is important to act deliberately to support every child's sense of self, including family and cultural bonds.

Respect the rights of young children. Allow children to engage in learner-centered free choice play, and to learn autonomy and freedom of choice. Support a sense of control by providing materials, toys, books, and experiences that incorporate their ideas, interests, and preferences. Thus, children learn about control, consequences of choice, sharing power, and other early principles of democracy.

Invest in caring and supportive relationships throughout the setting. All relationships with, between, and surrounding young children in a group setting impact healthy brain development and overall physical and psychological health and well-being (Bronfenbrenner & Morris 2006; NSCDC 2004; Shore 2003). Thus, all in the setting should commit to maintaining a positive emotional climate that models caring, positive, supportive communication and interaction.

Respond promptly and sensitively to children's communications. The sensitivity of caregivers' interactions and promptness is linked to the development of a secure attachment between children and adults in group settings, and to children's feelings of self-worth and trust. Thus, it is important for caregivers to get to know individual children well in order to respond appropriately and respectfully.

Understanding Changes in the First Three Years

Many variables impact the rapid changes that occur during the first three years. Families' beliefs and values about how to rear children interact with genetic makeup and numerous environmental factors. Who children are and who they become is determined by the interplay of all of these factors and the interactions and experiences they have during the first weeks, months, and years of life.

We describe the changes that occur in the brain and body from birth to 3 using terms including *growth, maturation,* and *development*, as well as *assimilation* and *accommodation*. These processes are highly interdependent, each influenced by and in turn influencing the others. We discuss each briefly below.

Growth, Maturation, and Development

Growth involves changes in the body in terms of amounts, such as size and weight, length/height, head circumference, and so on—mostly observable and easily measured factors. Growth occurs along with physical changes in internal organs and tissues, and their structures and functioning related to maturation.

Maturation refers to the timing and rates of change in how the body functions and is determined largely by biology. For instance, maturation determines the timing of when a toddler achieves bladder control.

Development accompanies growth and maturation but refers to changes from simple to increasingly complex ways of dealing with the world—for instance, in facing physical challenges, communicating, thinking and problem solving, and feeling about and relating to oneself and others. Outward behavioral expressions signal to caregivers that development has occurred. For example, infants develop the ability to distinguish people they know from ones they do not, and they might display stranger anxiety; toddlers now understand cause and effect, which adults know because they overhear them making predictions tied to recent events.

Assimilation and Accommodation

Another way that children change over the first three years is the development of how they think, process information, and learn. Piaget described the dual processes of assimilation and accommodation to help explain this (Piaget & Inhelder 1969). As infants and toddlers interact with those around them and engage with their environment, their minds are busy processing sensory input to make sense of the experiences. *Assimilation* occurs when encountering new information that fits with a structure already in place in the brain, which has stored information about prior knowledge or experiences very much like this new information. The brain simply adds this new information to the existing structure.

Accommodation occurs when new information that a child encounters is familiar enough that the existing structures in the brain can be reshaped and stretched to fit the new concept. Accommodation can occur only if the new information is not too different from what the child has already learned. Thus, the infant and toddler brain takes in information and learns by accumulating knowledge through assimilation. It is also ready to accommodate completely novel concepts and skills, as long as they relate in some way to prior knowledge and experience. If the new concept or skill the brain is asked to accommodate is too different from what the brain already knows (i.e., has a structure for), the brain cannot process it.

For example, an infant is presented with a bottle that is not her own and that has a nipple slightly different than she had before. Her brain has an existing structure for "this is a thing that holds my milk, and I suck on a nipple to get it." Her brain will make the shift to the new bottle and nipple quickly, adapting by assimilation and simply adding to her knowledge and experience more kinds of "things that hold my milk." Now, if sometime later her milk comes in a sippy cup instead of a bottle, her existing brain structure has to change, be completely altered—she must accommodate. Accommodation results in reshaping the existing knowledge and experience structure, resulting in the learning of something completely new: sipping rather than sucking to drink her milk.

The Environment

The nature-versus-nurture debate was settled long ago: who young children will be unfolds in constant interaction with the environment. What caregivers do—their interactions, the environments they set up, and the experiences they offer—impacts (both positively and negatively) young children's growth, maturation, and development, as well as their learning through assimilation and accommodation.

Observing Development From Birth to 3

The topics below respond to the question: "To be effective in their work with infants and toddlers, what do caregivers need to know about development in the first three years?" In some cases, the material provides guidance about what caregivers will be able to directly observe as children's development unfolds over time. In others, the information helps adults understand processes that impact the developing infant and toddler.

Despite the fact that no one area of development occurs in isolation, we identify five developmental domains to help organize and clarify understanding of the unique processes that occur within them. (See "Five Developmental Domains and Focus of Concentration" on p. 29.) Since development in any area occurs simultaneously with development in others and is *dependent* upon it, caregivers should look for areas of integration as they consider this material.

Caregivers can use the information to

• Focus their observations of the development of the children in their care

• Develop language to share information about children's development with families and document developmental profiles

• Create plans for individuals and groups related to expectations for potential next steps in healthy development

Five Developmental Domains and Focus of Concentration

Developmental Domain	Description	Focus of Concentration for Observation and Planning

Physical Growth and Development of Habits for Lifetime Wellness and Safe Living	**Physical health and growth:** includes observing height and weight, adequate and proper nutrition, signs of abuse, chronic illnesses, or injuries; **psychological well-being:** looking at stress level at home and in group care; modeling and teaching **healthy and safe habits** and growth in capacity for **self-care** relate to developing personal caregiving and learning to take charge of own care needs.	Physical health and growth
		Psychological health and well-being
		    Infant mental health
		    Emotional climates
		    Child abuse and neglect
		Learning to be healthy and safe
		Self-care

Thinking, Reasoning and Understanding the World: The Brain and Cognitive Development	**Cognitive development** refers to both the acquisition of knowledge and changes in intellectual processes that impact infants' and toddlers' understanding about the world; the ability and complexity to think, reason, and problem solve changes over time through early experiences.	Growing brain and experience
		Cognitive processes
		    Focus and attention
		    Object permanence
		    Cause and effect
		    Sorting and classifying
		    Memory, imitation, and recall

The Mind–Body Connection: Development of Sensorimotor Integration	**Perceptual development** occurs as infants and toddlers use all their senses to explore their environment. **Motor development** involves ongoing refinement of small (fine) and large (gross) muscles, with the child becoming increasingly able to coordinate, balance, and control her body.	Perceptual development Motor development Spatial awareness

Being and Belonging: Social and Emotional Development	**Social development** is understanding of oneself as an individual and a growing awareness of others. **Emotional development** refers to understanding/labeling feelings, knowing that others possess them, and learning how to regulate them; **moral sense**, including knowing right from wrong, caring for others, and empathy; and an **aesthetic sense** of the world—what is beautiful, what young children appreciate, and why.	Sense of self and others
		Self-confidence and self-esteem
		Interacting with others
		    Temperament
		    Peer interactions
		Prosocial behaviors
		Emotional development
		Attachment
		Emotional regulation

Communication: Development of Language, Literacy, and Mathematical Understanding	**Language development** involves **receptive language and listening** (understanding what is said, verbally or not) and **expressive language** (being able to communicate to be understood), both of which are necessary for understanding and using symbols for **literacy and mathematical understanding**—being able to recognize that words, signs, and symbols have meaning, and to use them.	Receptive language and listening Expressive language Early literacy and mathematical understanding

Adapted from CDE (2009) and Shonkoff and Phillips (2000).

Physical Growth and Development of Habits for Lifetime Wellness and Safe Living

Over the first three years of life, the body changes more than at any other time. A healthy start can set a child on a trajectory of physical and psychological wellness for life. Some families may need assistance in identifying and connecting with resources and services to help with health and wellness issues. Family-centered programs have a role in working with families to engage in this process.

A Caution About Milestones

Development during the first three years occurs in a fairly predictable and orderly sequence, but at different rates for individual children. It is important for caregivers not to overinterpret information from tables of ages and stages for developmental benchmarks found in parenting books, pediatricians' offices, on the web, or even included in this chapter.

Caregivers can think of developmental milestones as achievements to celebrate with infants and toddlers when reached, rather than deficits or marks of failure if they do not hit the average time for benchmarks. It is common for young children to develop more quickly in some areas than in others. Caregivers can assist families in interpreting such information and help prevent them from becoming anxious.

Having general expectations for development is helpful to caregivers, however, in uncovering potential problems that might result in developmental delays. Caregivers should be on alert for children who, in their experience, seem to be taking an exceptionally long time to develop in one or more areas. If caregivers notice patterns of exceptionalities over time, they can discuss these patterns with families, and then support families if and when they seek further evaluation from other professionals (Elicker & McMullen 2013). Be sure to keep children's birth histories in mind, however, as premature infants—especially those with very low birth weights—can take longer to reach milestones for their calendar age.

Physical Health and Growth

During his first year, an infant might triple his birth weight and add between six and nine inches in height. Although the growth rate slows the second year, by age 2 a child might grow another three to five inches and quadruple his birth weight. It is important that health care professionals monitor this tremendously fast growth carefully.

Adequate and proper nutrition is essential to health during the rapid growth of the first three years. It is critical for caregivers to follow all nutritional guidelines, and to be in full agreement with families—who should be working closely with health care providers—when making decisions about how best to meet children's nutritional needs in the group setting.

Sleep is as important to health as adequate nutrition. The amount of sleep infants and toddlers need varies greatly, and young infants, at least, should always be allowed to follow their own napping schedule. By the time children enter their second year in group care, most can follow a naptime routine that is consistent with others in the group, as long as those who need to are allowed to catnap at other times. The sleep of young children should be respected as a developmental need, and effort should be made to provide a comfortable and restful nap area. Place cribs as far from the general play area as possible, in an area where lights can be dimmed and the noise level lessened.

Psychological Health and Well-Being

The field of infant mental health research and practice has taught us much about the importance of the relationship between stress in young children and their families and its impact on children's development. Attachment issues between family and child; alcoholism and drug abuse in the home; neglect or abuse of the child; spousal abuse; parental imprisonment; maternal depression; and generally negative emotional climates in the home can impact the emotional well-being and subsequent development of young children.

Even stressors that are not as extreme can impact a child's health and well-being. Caregivers may notice a healthy and active child become suddenly withdrawn, disinterested, or lethargic. Or a child might become hyperactive, reacting to every slight change. A stressed child might exhibit radical changes in sleeping, eating, or elimination patterns. The main symptom is radical change—they are simply not acting like themselves.

Stress and other signs of lack of emotional well-being, such as general unhappiness, should be taken seriously and discussed with the family to consider how best to support both child and family. Regardless of children's level of stress, group care settings should strive to be free from undue stress for children and their families, who need to feel the group care environment is a place of calmness, security, trust, and above all safety.

Issues around the highly intimate physical caregiving routines associated with feeding/eating, diapering/toileting, sleeping, and dressing, and when (or if) to foster independence, are bound in culture, tradition, and family values, requiring caregivers to be open and sensitive to differences in families' belief systems and cultures. Conflicts that sometimes emerge around these issues can be very stressful for all, and ultimately detrimental to a child's developing sense of identity. It is important for adults to be diligent in reflecting on their own beliefs at these times, making sure their biases and values do not dictate responses to families and behaviors with infants and toddlers, but rather rational, well-reasoned thought prevails.

Learning to Be Healthy and Safe

One additional principle could have been added to the seven described earlier: do no harm. Of course, all caregivers live by this already. Everything adults do in the birth-to-3 setting is done first and foremost to ensure that infants and toddlers remain healthy and safe. Caregivers engage in a thousand practices daily they hardly give thought to—such as following fire codes, childproofing the rooms, checking the play yard for harmful substances, using appropriately mixed cleaning fluids, and wearing gloves to change diapers—all to ensure the health and safety of those in their care. They want infants and toddlers to live and play, learn and develop, in a healthy and safe environment.

As caregivers go about their day engaging in healthy and safe practices, they are modeling those practices as well as personal wellness habits. What caregivers do in the presence of children—eating apples for a snack, hand washing throughout the day, taking a walk in the sunshine on their break, looking both ways before crossing a street—provides a model for young children about health, safety, and taking care of oneself.

Self-Care

By the end of the first three years, infants and toddlers grow in their capacity to help caregivers with routines and even take charge over some personal needs themselves. Many 4- and 5-month-olds cooperate during diaper changing, holding clean diapers and wet wipes, positioning their bodies for the adult. Most mobile infants can identify their own belongings, and help get shoes, boots, coats, and other clothing on by extending their arms and legs as needed. Toddlers can easily undress themselves and some can put on a jacket, but probably not zip or button it. They can also brush their hair and teeth, with some assistance.

The ability to eat independently advances quickly, beginning at around 8 months. But just because a child can do something does not always mean it should be encouraged. Independence in general—and specifically in feeding/eating—is culturally bound, and caregivers must consider carefully their snack and mealtime practices in the context of families. Many families and cultures value interdependence over independence. Partnering with families around goals for each child helps caregivers know when to encourage independence.

Thinking, Reasoning, and Understanding the World: The Brain and Cognitive Development

Cognitive development, which is dependent upon having a healthy brain, refers primarily to intellectual development—the ability for young children to grow in their capacity to make sense of the world around them. As infants and toddlers learn with ever-increasing ability and complexity, they develop how they think, reason, and problem solve.

The Growing Brain and Experience

The overall rate of development in all domains from birth to age 3 is greater than at any other time in life, and this is no more remarkable than when looking at brain development. By the age of 2, the brain grows from about three-quarters of a pound to about two-and-a-half pounds, nearly its full adult weight of about three pounds. At birth, babies have more than 100 billion nerve cells, or neurons, which are all that are needed for living. But to grow, the brain needs to make connections between those neurons and build pathways through the brain. By the end of the first month of life, a healthy brain makes

100 trillion connections between and among neurons—connections made as the infant interacts with and is responded to by adults (NSCDC 2004; Shonkoff & Phillips 2000).

The brain makes more neural connections by age 3 than at any other time in life. These connections are not all equally strong or necessary for survival or well-being, and many wither and die. However, those formed by repeated experience or strong emotion—positive and negative—grow stronger and thrive. Brain research now supports what early childhood educators concluded long ago—that it is the quality of the environment, of early experiences, and of relationships that is the most critical contributor to ensuring strong, healthy developmental outcomes for infants and toddlers (NSCDC 2004; Shonkoff & Phillips 2000; Shore 2003).

Growing and nurturing a healthy brain requires proper nutrition, sleep, healthy environments free of toxins, and well-baby checkups. We also know that in group settings, healthy brain development depends upon children's positive relationships with caregivers who know them well and who provide experiences that inspire, challenge, and ignite the brain's neurons and reinforce neural pathways. Healthy brain development is critical to all of the cognitive processes that will be described in the next sections, and is particularly important to the development of memory—the ability to store, recall, and utilize information—which is central to being able to learn and build upon prior experience.

Cognitive Processes for Making Sense of the World

Cognitive development allows the growing infant and toddler to continue to gain knowledge, and increase the complexity and efficiency in how they think about and process information. The cognitive achievements unfold in behaviors that caregivers can observe and support, as discussed in this section.

Focus and attention. The ability to focus attention is a critical cognitive skill related to learning that begins in earliest infancy. In the first hours after birth, healthy newborn babies are often highly alert and will turn toward sounds (usually voices) that attract their attention. They show preference for certain voices, preferring their mother's voice to those of any other person, distinguishing it from any other female because it is her voice that they heard while in the womb. Some newborns can also single out their father's voice from other male voices, although only if the father has been present and highly verbal with the mother throughout the pregnancy (Lee 2010).

These early signs that infants want attention and are ready to give it set the scene for face-to-face interactions with adults. The responses draw adults in and aid in the bonding between newborn and parents, launching them on the road to what will hopefully be a relationship based upon a strong and secure attachment. Gaining the attention of infants, and later toddlers, is essential in establishing relationships that allow us to support healthy overall growth and development, but it also helps them develop the skills of focusing attention.

Sometime after about the first six weeks and continuing throughout infancy, babies become drawn to human faces, seeming to find them fascinating. They attend to changes in faces: smiles, frowns, the ways eyebrows move up and down. Caregivers who pay careful attention will see their own expressions mirrored on those of infants as they look back at them. It is important to allow babies to have face-to-face time, to have plenty of these early private conversations, examining each others' faces—they coo, you coo; they smile, you smile. These early exchanges also teach infants about language and communication, how to recognize the emotions of others, and build their feelings of self-worth as persons valued as relationship partners.

Around 8 to 10 months, most infants are able to follow a line of sight, or focus on something brought to their attention just from someone else's eye gaze. This becomes more sophisticated sometime around 10 to 14 months, when mobile infants become capable of engaging in joint attention with others. *Joint attention* occurs when two people share focus on one object or event. Adults will notice that a child is looking at something, and he may even point to something and enjoy regarding this object. These behaviors signal the child is cognitively at a point where the caregiver can now draw his attention more readily to focus on aspects of experiences they are sharing. These skills are critical in the infant's development of intention and reference, which when combined with words and environmental symbols, prepare them for both spoken language and literacy acquisition (Bruner 1985).

Infants' attention skills allow them to focus on what caregivers say and show them, despite the many distractions in group care. They begin to be able to sit in the caregiver's lap (for short periods, at least), to enjoy a board book, or to crawl or toddle over to hear a group of friends clapping and dancing to music. Soon, their ability to sit and focus on book reading extends longer and longer.

Two-year-olds will demonstrate they have listened to songs, rhymes, favorite books, and oft-repeated chants by correcting caregivers, sometimes even becoming upset when caregivers recite them "wrong" or differently than expected. As frustrating as this may sometimes be to adults it is a cognitive advancement to be respected, one to reframe as an accomplishment and to look upon with a source of pride in the work you have done with the young children in your care.

Object permanence. *Object permanence* involves the ability to hold a mental image or picture of an object or person in the mind, and to understand that when that object or person is out of sight or beyond hearing, it continues to exist. This has important implications for how young children explore, how they understand their environments, for memory, and for issues such as separation and stranger anxiety.

It is thought that newborns have no understanding that they are separate and apart from everything else in the world—that they are one with everything else (Berk 2012). At about 1 to 4 months, infants develop the ability to follow with their eyes, or track, objects as they move into their field of vision. At the same time, they show the first signs of developing object permanence, as they will continue to look for the object for a few seconds after it disappears from view. For the most part, however, it is common to characterize young infants' understanding of objects as "out of sight, out of mind."

At 4 to 8 months, infants have increasing experiences with objects—toys, books, people—in their environments. They engage in both assimilation and accommodation as they explore, making cognitive advances in object understanding. Caregivers will notice them reach for objects, even ones that are partially hidden or covered. Infants are now able to hold objects and events in memory, although only for a short time.

With the development of being able to remember objects and people who are no longer present may

come behaviors such as infants becoming upset when an adult leaves their sight. This behavior, known as *separation anxiety,* signals a cognitive advancement but also means the infant lacks the cognitive capacity to understand that when someone is out of sight, they still exist and will return. Separation anxiety improves with repeat experience and sensitive reassurance.

At 7 or 8 months, infants are less likely to have significant separation anxiety, but a new fear may emerge as a result of this cognitive advancement: stranger anxiety. The early months spent focusing on faces and new increased memory capacity come together for young children, who can now identify and remember the people they love and trust most, and to notice—and sometimes fear—unfamiliar people. Also around this time, caregivers might notice that toddlers will follow a ball that rolls completely out of sight or search for a toy that is completely hidden. This behavior signals that they understand that objects continue to exist when they are out of view and that they are able to predict to some extent where they will be. After 12 months, understanding of objects develops rapidly. By the time they are 2, toddlers can search for and retrieve hidden objects, hunting with focus and persistence for missing toys, almost obsessively so at times!

Cause and effect. *Cause and effect* is the understanding that one action or event results in another, which—along with the development of memory and understanding of objects—is critical in being able to make predictions, reason, and problem solve effectively. Cause and effect is learned by experimenting and playing with objects in the environment.

Between 1 and 4 months of age, infants spend most of their time seeing, listening, and learning about things that happen around them, but not really connecting that any specific behavior or action causes any specific response or reaction (CDE 2009; Marotz & Allen 2012). Infants' brains and bodies are very active at this time, however. Their arms and legs move about and interact with objects; they make noises; things move when they swipe or kick them; they make faces and sounds and others react. Infants begin to take notice and they make connections: "I made that happen."

After about 4 months, infants begin making simple, purposeful actions to elicit responses. They find that when they bang a cup on a tray, it makes a loud sound; kicking their legs makes the bells on their shoes sing out; and slapping water with their hands in the tub results in a delightful splash. In addition, they begin to notice that caregivers cause things to happen. Their caregiver punches a button and music starts. Not only do they notice, but infants will begin to let adults know that they want them to repeat actions that they find desirable.

The 7- or 8-month-old becomes expert in experimenting with her newfound understanding of causality. By about 12 months, she will be able to combine many simple actions together to solve simple sensorimotor problems. For example, if a toy is out of reach but on a blanket, she will pull the blanket closer to her to gain access to the toy. She experiments with different objects— a wooden spoon, stick, toy hammer—to see which makes the loudest sound when pounded on a pot or pan.

Two-year-olds are very adept at using cause and effect in their explorations and problem solving. Improving cognition allows them to make predictions about what might happen. Increased memory capacity allows them to reflect on why things happened based on their understanding of how things work.

Sorting and classifying. Part of understanding how things work in the world depends on the ability to organize information, to sort and categorize it in some way. This critical skill begins developing in the first three years and is important for being able to use symbols to read and perform mathematics in the future. Sorting and classifying objects, experiences, and people is neces- sary for forming expectations and making predictions—vital skills for becom- ing good problem solvers and for negotiating complex social relationships.

The first milestone in developing sorting and classification skills comes when infants learn to distinguish people from inanimate objects. Young infants will demonstrate they have clearly different expectations for the people around them than for the other "things" in their environment. By 3 or 4 months, infants have essentially sorted out two large categories—alive and not alive. Through the next months, they will learn to distinguish familiar from unfamiliar objects and people they know from those they do not.

Between about 8 and 18 months, children not only notice novel objects, but they begin to sort out how things are similar and different, a major cogni- tive achievement. Using their new abilities to focus and attend, they notice particular attributes of objects and people, which allows them to separate them into at least two categories based upon one significant and prominent characteristic. This helps them identify, for example, things that make noise versus those that do not, and things they can ride, or push, or pull versus toys that are not so action oriented.

Caregivers may see one child quietly picking all the blue beads out of a jar, or another pulling all the trucks from a basket of vehicles. In each case, the child has focused on one attribute that sets the items apart from the others. A child will sometimes lose track of the attribute they were focusing on and switch to another. For example, a caregiver watches as a 10-month-old girl pulls animals out of the toy basket one at a time, lining them up on the floor. After lining up four toy animals, she adds a fifth that is a horse, which catches her attention. The next several items she lines up are horses from around the room. The category she uses for sorting shifts, but she still remains focused on one attribute: first it was sorting animals from all other toys, then it was horses.

Toddlers rapidly become more sophisticated at sorting and classifying. They can create multiple piles of objects based upon one attribute, but still only one. For example, a 2-year-old girl plays with beads that are all the same size but have different colors. The caregiver looks over to find she has become quietly absorbed in pulling out all the blue beads and setting them aside in one pile, the yellow in another, and the green and red in two other groups. She is sorting by one attribute (color), but she can look at multiple colors.

Memory, imitation, and recall. Memory is a complex process that develops along with brain development. Babies are born with a *working memory,* which allows for representations to be held in the mind for a matter of seconds (Berk 2012). For example, a newborn in the highly alert state soon after birth imitates the facial expressions of an adult 30 seconds after the interaction. Throughout infancy this early type of memory is at work, allowing infants to mirror the eyebrow raising, eye squinting, mouth shapes and tonguing, and smiles and frowns they see in face-to-face conversations.

Long-term memory involves the storage of information over time so that it can be recalled as needed. Long-term memory has two types: implicit and explicit. *Implicit long-term memories* are those related to certain concepts and skills and are collected through daily experiences. Examples of implicit memory include using knowledge of objects to know "my favorite toy must be here somewhere, I just have to look"; and using stored muscle movement and balance memory to roll a ball back to an adult. These memories are not retrieved consciously; they are not accessible for recall in the usual sense—they are just there. *Explicit long-term memories* are what most people think of as memory. They are our thoughts about people we know, past experiences, and knowledge and skills learned.

Many people remember very little about their lives from before they were 3 due to *infantile amnesia.* Many memories from those years are highly unstable, especially until age 2 or so, and are not subject to explicit memory. Infants are, however, storing many important implicit long-term memories. Also, because the brain undergoes such massive pruning of early neural connections, much of what infants store in explicit memory might be lost or simply difficult to retrieve from stored memory.

Current research confirms that infants as young as 6 months can start forming stable explicit memories, being able to recall actions from 24 hours in the past. Just as the brain develops rapidly, so does this aspect of useful memory ability. By 9 months an infant can reliably recall information from up to one month in the past, and by 20 months she can remember events that happened up to a year earlier (Bauer & Pathman 2008). Thus, the older the child gets, the better and more reliable the ability to remember and recall memories becomes.

The Mind–Body Connection: Development of Sensorimotor Integration

The systems in the brain that control the senses—vision, hearing, smell, taste, touch, and proprioception (the sense of one's body in space)—develop in full integration with the systems of the brain that control large and small muscle growth and development. As senses develop, infants and then toddlers use their bodies as a means to explore, reach out, and make sense of the world— hence, the term *sensorimotor,* or *sensory integration* (Shonkoff & Phillips 2000; Shore 2003). Through sensory integration, young children develop the ability to control and coordinate their muscles and balance, skills essential to achieving true goal-directed behavior.

Perceptual Development

Healthy *perceptual development* is concerned with how infants and toddlers process sensory information through experiences and interactions with objects and people in their environment. A newborn is ready, literally from the moment of birth, to make sense of the world.

Newborns' senses of taste, hearing, and smell develop before birth and are quite acute. Their sense of smell is so strong that they can distinguish their mother's breast milk from any other. As mentioned earlier, they can distinguish their parents' voices from those of other adults. Newborns' vision, unlike these other senses, has limited capability at birth. A "hidden" sense, known as *proprioception*, also develops in the womb: as fetuses kick their legs and wave their arms they begin the journey toward developing a sense of position, an understanding of how their bodies move in space.

For the first few weeks of life, infants typically have clear vision for objects and faces within 8 to 12 inches, just the distance needed to see their parents' faces. Beyond this distance vision is hazy, and because they are born with some light sensitivity, colors appear washed out. The newborn can, however, focus attention on a toy or small object held in front of them and moved horizontally across their field of vision. By 3 or 4 months, vision, depth perception, and the ability to see all colors improve to the point that most infants can see clearly and in full color across a room. They can also track objects with their eyes, moving up and down as well as horizontally across their line of sight.

The brain allows for all the senses to be working at the same time, and most infants can process sensory input from many sources all at once, but caregivers should be alert for children who are overloaded by the sights, sounds, and smells around them. Some young infants will simply shut down, turn away, or fall fast asleep when sensory input becomes too much for them to handle, whereas others will become highly disturbed and anxious. Mobile infants and toddlers can also become overstimulated, sometimes appearing confused or even dissolving into tears or acting out in inappropriate ways because they simply do not know how to handle all the input coming at them so rapidly. Knowing the individual children in our care well and being able to modify physical aspects of the environment to meet their needs is critical. Noise level, clutter, smells, or lighting may need to be adjusted. Through interaction and experience, caregivers will become in tune with children's cues about sensitivities to differing sensory stimuli and how best to respond (Elicker, Fortner-Wood, & Noppe 1999; Lally & Mangione 2008).

Motor Development

Fine and gross motor development occurs as the body grows physically, in a process called *motor development,* emphasizing that it is all about movement. Fine motor skills relate to the small muscles of the body (e.g., in the fingers, toes, and lips), whereas gross motor activity requires development of the large muscles (e.g., in the arms and legs). Controlling muscles at will, balancing, and coordination are key developments in birth to 3 that allow young infants to roll over, start crawling, and grasp a toy; allow mobile infants to take their first steps and feed themselves with relative ease; and allow toddlers to run and jump, turn pages in a book, and finger-paint.

Healthy motor development, like all development, begins long before birth. As fetuses swim within the confines of the uterus, they exercise muscles and build connections in the brain about how it feels to move. For the early months of life, infants kick their legs, move their arms about, and rotate their heads from side to side, and can even lift their head up a bit for short periods of time.

Most young infants' movements are random and not under their control, but they also are endowed at birth with certain reflexes that help jump-start the building and strengthening of the mind–body connection. These reflexes are inborn ways of responding and moving that the infant is pre-wired to do; they build and strengthen neural pathways to facilitate the learning of behaviors that are necessary for survival. For instance, the rooting reflex helps the newborn find the nipple of a breast or bottle, and then the sucking reflex engages so they can be nourished right after birth.

Many of these important reflexes still exist at 6 or 8 weeks, the earliest we might see young infants in group care. The reflexes and random, accidental movements are important stepping stones upon which all future motor control—and thus the ability to integrate sensory information—is built. Consider, for example

- A young infant reflexively grasps her caregiver's finger; her caregiver smiles at her and says something; the infant finds this pleasurable

- An infant in his stroller flails his arms about randomly, just having fun; his hands hit a toy that moves around and gets his attention; after several stroller rides and several random arm movements, the toy moves again

In both of these cases, the stage is set for the infants to develop control of the muscles involved in these experiences. The brain made connections between what the infants sensed—feeling the caregiver's finger, hearing the nice tone in his voice, seeing the toy move—and the muscular movement related to those pleasurable outcomes. It just takes time and lots of repeat experience to strengthen the neural pathways of the brain related to these processes.

Spatial Awareness

Understanding spatial awareness is necessary for children under 3 to know how to make their bodies move to get from here to there; to figure out what to do with their bodies to retrieve a toy that is just out of reach; to remember where the little room with the potty is in relation to the play area; to decide how far away or nearby an object or another person is to them; and to determine how fast objects (including themselves) are moving. The development of spatial understanding occurs through repeated experiences involving the perceptual and motor systems working in harmony, primarily through sensorimotor play.

Spatial understanding is an important development for later academic learning. It is fundamental to being able to structure and organize written work, and it is connected to preparing the brain to solve more complex mathematical and logic problems. Birth-to-3 caregivers can support the development of conceptual understanding related to spatial awareness by using and reinforcing words related to position and place, such as *up, down, slow, fast, here, there, over, under, right, left, back, forth, first,* and *last.*

Being and Belonging: Social and Emotional Development

Social and emotional development are closely intertwined. Feelings young children have about themselves and others greatly affect whether or not they will engage socially, and social interactions in turn influence emotions. *Social development* involves the growing understanding of oneself as apart from and in interaction with others, whereas *emotional development* involves understanding and managing feelings about oneself, others, and the world.

Birth-to-3 caregivers concentrate on social and emotional development, long recognized in the field of early childhood education as foundational to ensuring positive outcomes. It relates to who children are now and who they will be in the future as successful learners, responsible citizens, and happy, well-adjusted people (Honig 2002; Hyson 2004). The topics below describe the complex social and emotional lives of infants and toddlers that adults can consider as they observe, plan, and support children's developing emotional and social competence.

Sense of Self and Others

Sense of self refers to the awareness of who we are—our identity—in relation to others. Research suggests that newborns have no sense of self (Berk 2012; Eisenberg & Mussen 1989). For the first few weeks of life, they are often characterized as "being at one with the universe," in that they have no sense of themselves apart from anything else in their environment. Within a few weeks however, they have sorted out who their parents and/or primary attachment figures are, and to feel at one with them—there is my parent/my primary caregiver and me (as one unit), and then there is everyone else.

At around 4 months infants have enough experience, and their understanding of objects has developed sufficiently for them to know they are separate from their parent/primary caregiver. Yet their parent/primary caregiver is the source of all security and trust for the infant, the infant's greatest developmental need and focus at this time. Because of this dependency (and continued advancement in object knowledge), separation anxiety might emerge. The awakening realization that they and their parent/primary caregiver together are not one, but separate, coupled with the disappearance of that person from time to time, can be confusing and emotionally unsettling.

The 8- and 9-month-old infant takes off crawling and then walking, engaging busily in sensorimotor exploration and rather preoccupied in doing so. She might display signs of stranger anxiety or show mild wariness or even curiosity toward new people, as she is now able to sort people as (1) me; (2) my parent/primary caregiver; (3) people I know; and (4) people I do not know.

Toddlers begin exhibiting behaviors that demonstrate an emergence of true self-identity. They are known to claim their independence, even at times when autonomy is not granted or appropriate, through the expression of strong emotions, opinions, preferences, desires, and needs. At the same time that toddlers become more aware of their individuality (and are increasingly capable of expressing it!), they also become more socially aware and capable of caring for and about those around them. They develop a sense of belonging to their caregiving group and to their family. They know the members of their caregiving group and show strong group affiliation, demonstrating preference for particular friends. Also, they enjoy looking at and showing pictures of their family members.

Self-Confidence and Self-Esteem

Self-confidence and self-esteem are two separate concepts, often spoken of together. To be *self-confident,* a person must believe without a doubt they are capable of doing something successfully. The toddler who is self-confident she is an artist will not hesitate at the easel—she will select her brush and quickly begin painting. The mobile infant who is self-confident about climbing will push his caregiver's hands away as he walks up the steps of the slide. The young infant who is self-confident about her balance will sit upright for the first time on her own. Success builds success, and success builds confidence. Self-confidence will endure failures and frustration, as long as they are not constant.

Self-esteem addresses how a person regards or approves of himself, or more simply, whether one likes or loves himself. Young children receive critical messages from caregivers about whether or not they are lovable, or if they and their families are acceptable, and that impacts the formation of self-esteem.

For toddlers, self-esteem can be complicated because they are increasingly more socially engaged. They are also developing more sophistication in terms of *theory of mind*—the ability to understand that other people have thoughts, beliefs, intentions, and feelings, and that they may be different from our own (Flavell & Hartman 2004). The 2- to 3-year-old becomes aware that, just as she forms ideas and opinions about her peers, they form opinions about her.

It is important to consider both self-confidence and self-esteem in the context of culture. Discuss with families whether and how to encourage self-confidence or self-esteem in their children. For instance, some cultures value the esteem of others over self-esteem. Others may be worried that a child encouraged to become highly self-confident may become too boastful or perhaps too independent.

Interacting With Others

As soon as infants master cause and effect, they understand that if they behave in a certain way or attempt to communicate, it might elicit a response. They have numerous face-to-face interactions with their caregivers in which they learn the comfortable back-and-forth rhythm of conversation. As mobile infants begin to motor about, they quickly learn that other behaviors elicit reactions, sometimes negative responses. Soon the child figures out that the responses and reactions were related to what he did. It is through these experiences that toddlers deepen their understanding that things they do in a social group elicit reactions, and thus what they do and say when among others has consequences—a key social achievement.

Temperament. Young children's environment, and the responses and reactions of those within it, shapes infants' and toddlers' early social communications and behaviors. It is important for adults who work with birth-to-3 groups to understand the influence of temperament on social behaviors.

Temperament describes the characteristic way in which individuals— children and adults—interact with the world. Everyone is born with a temperament, which interacts with the environment to shape the developing personality. Understanding the temperaments of all young children in a group can help caregivers guide early social interactions. Caregivers need to be aware of their own temperaments and how their characteristic ways of responding might be in tune with or at odds with other group members. It is the responsibility of adults to adjust their styles to fit and respond appropriately to infants and toddlers, not the other way around.

Temperament includes a number of traits, and all individuals lie somewhere within these extremes:

- Activity level—is highly active or calm and relaxed

- Rhythm—has regular or erratic body functions (e.g., eating, sleeping, elimination)

- Approach/withdrawal—adjusts easily to new people or experiences or does not

- Adaptability—adjusts to changes and transitions easily or resists and has difficulty

- Intensity—reacts strongly (positively or negatively) or calmly and quietly to situations

- Mood—tends to have a strong negative or positive outlook, or is more even tempered

- Persistence—sticks to a task even if it becomes difficult, or gives up easily

- Distractibility—is easily distracted or can easily block out external stimuli

- Sensory threshold—is bothered or not by certain sensory stimuli (e.g., noise, light, certain clothing textures)

Caregivers are familiar with most temperament types—easy/flexible, slow to warm up, difficult/feisty—and they can use this information to understand and plan for individual children, as well as to facilitate social interactions in the group. It is important, though, to avoid labeling children and to consider the categories more specifically for individual infants and toddlers.

Peer interactions. In group settings, children as young as 3 months can have positive peer interactions. Mobile infants might have clear friendship preferences, although it is more common after age 2 (Riley et al. 2008). Friends are important to the development of children's emotional well-being and in working out social difficulties. These relationships develop over time. Young infants start paying attention and showing interest to peers when they arrive to the group care setting. Mobile infants might get particularly excited when special buddies arrive in the morning, even if they rarely play with them. Toddlers will notice and miss friends who are absent.

Toddlers develop the ability to initiate and respond to social overtures. They begin by enjoying playing near each other or side by side. Over time, back-and-forth interactions and exchanges of toys and communication increases, and ultimately pairs and groups begin to play cooperatively with one another. Negotiating social relationships and playing with friends is very different than the largely independent sensorimotor explorations of toddlerhood. These new social engagements are often fraught with emotion, and hurt or confused feelings. Interacting with peers has to be learned over time under the guidance of patient caregivers willing to reinforce some of the same lessons over and over again.

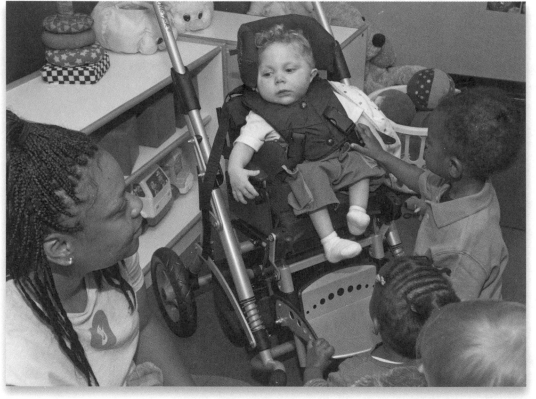

Prosocial Behaviors

Learning to engage in prosocial versus antisocial behaviors is a component of being able to make friends, being accepted by others in the group, and developing as a socially competent person. Young children in group settings are prosocial when "communications and behaviors on the part of a baby that help create a positive emotional climate in the group and that involve reaching out—positive, discernible, outward social expression on the part of one baby toward one or more other individuals, whether infant or adult" (McMullen et al. 2009, 21). Highly valued prosocial behaviors in birth-to-3 groups include caring, friendship, compassion, empathy, sharing, cooperation, turn taking, fairness, affection, listening, helping, kindness, and honesty.

For infants and toddlers to develop prosocial skills, they must first be cared for by respectful, caring adults who demonstrate these behaviors in all they do. Infants learn their first lessons of being a caring person by how they are cared for (Eisenberg & Mussen 1989; Noddings 2003). They learn how to receive and then return caring responses through those important back-and-forth, reciprocal exchanges with sensitive caregivers. By being treated with respect by adults, infants learn they are valued and, in turn, how to value and respect others.

Learning to be respectful of others, to truly appreciate and value other people, is critical for acquiring empathy. Quann and Wien (2006) define empathy in young children as "the capacity to observe the feelings of another and to respond with care and concern for that other" (22). Mobile infants become increasingly sophisticated in being able to first understand their own emotions, and then share in the emotional experience of others (Gordon 2009). Caregivers will know a child has developed this capability when they observe, for instance, a mobile infant trying to give a dropped toy back to a distraught young infant, or a toddler hugging a crying friend. Prosocial development and empathy are essential components in young children's growing sense of what is right and wrong, good and bad, and taking care of others, all components of learning what it means to be human and live in a community.

Emotional Development

Emotional development involves the feelings that infants and toddlers develop about themselves, others, and the world around them. Major developmental tasks in birth to 3 include developing a sense of security and trust, coming to understand emotions and labeling or naming feelings, and ultimately developing emotional regulation and learning to manage emotions, especially very strong ones. Closely tied to emotional development is a growing awareness of details of the wider world, part of the development of aesthetic sense, which includes developing a concept for beauty—understanding that they find some things more pleasurable or attractive than other things.

Attachment

The principles outlined earlier for developmentally appropriate practice in birth to 3 ("Guiding Principles of Practice," p. 26) are relationship based, meaning they are best accomplished in the context of strong, supportive relationships. The first and most important relationships infants form is with their "attachment figure(s)," one or more people with whom they will form a close, emotional bond in a relationship meant to last for a relatively long time. These relationships promote security and trust, which are essential for healthy emotional development. Secure attachments have been connected to social-emotional health and well-being, healthy brain development, social competency, and self-confidence, among other positive outcomes (Honig 2002; Raikes & Edwards 2009).

Infants and toddlers can form secure attachments to more than one attachment figure (e.g., parents and caregiver) without disrupting the bonds between parent and child. Being sensitive and prompt contributes to the development of a secure attachment between young children and their caregivers in group settings, and to their feelings of self-worth and trust (Lally & Mangione 2008; Mann & Carney 2008). However, constantly changing caregivers and breaking those intimate bonds jeopardize children's feelings of security and trust. To help ensure the close relationships that lead to children's security and trust, it is important to set up systems that ensure continuity of care and to assign a primary caregiver to individual children and families (Lally & Mangione 2008; Raikes & Edwards 2009).

Emotional Regulation

Emotional regulation begins developing in infancy and involves the increasing ability to wait patiently for needs to be met, to keep from acting impulsively in socially inappropriate ways, and to manage strong emotions. It is not about controlling emotions but developing an understanding of how to express them appropriately (Hyson 2004). These skills promote overall emotional regulation as well as competence. Central to a caregivers' role is helping babies learn what is socially acceptable for expressing various emotions and providing the words to label their feelings. Long before an infant can articulate an emotion verbally, a sensitive caregiver, in tune with the child emotionally, can provide the words to help young children internalize the meanings for concepts such as happy, angry, sad, and so on.

Caregivers support development of self-regulation by responding promptly and sensitively to young children's needs. Infants and toddlers who consistently have their needs met develop ways to self-soothe (learning to delay gratification) on those occasions when they have to wait, confident their trusted caregiver will come. The anxious child—the one who cannot predict when or if there will be a response—is delayed in self-regulating. Children with insecure (avoidant) attachments with parents have more difficulty learning to self-regulate, as do those who are more intense temperamentally.

Communication: Development of Language, Literacy, and Mathematical Understanding

Over the first three years, children rapidly learn to understand the meaning of language and to use both verbal and nonverbal communication. Understanding language and being an effective communicator are precursors to skills needed for understanding and using symbols to convey meaning.

Receptive Language and Listening

Receptive language refers to a child's understanding of the meaning of a message being given, usually through spoken language or signing. Caregivers can also communicate with young children through music or rhythms, which can convey moods or feelings. Infants begin processing sounds well before birth, due to their well-developed sense of hearing and their developing perceptual abilities. And although this is later lost, the newborn brain's pre-wiring of sensory neurons gives them the ability to hear all phonemes (the smallest, most basic units of sound in a language) present in all human languages—they are ready to be born into any family, any place on earth and begin acquiring language (Bjorklund 2011).

Infants bathed in speech and language sounds build an understanding for language quickly. Talking to and with infants and toddlers about what is happening in the environment, asking for their cooperation, chatting with them during caregiving routines, and identifying objects clearly by name are effective methods for building receptive vocabulary. Similarly, reading picture books and poetry, singing, and rhyming teach cadence and context for words and how they fit together in patterns.

Estimates of how many words babies know before they begin speaking vary widely, but we know that they understand far more than they can say. An infant as young as 4 months can understand the word *no* when clearly spoken to them with a stern face. Eight-month-olds pay increasing attention to speech, often listening very hard to what is being said, and they can now sort out their home language from others.

Between 8 and 18 months, children recognize names for many familiar objects (e.g., ball, keys, doggy) and can follow simple directions such as "Give me your cup, please" or "Show me your belly button!" By 18 months, they are thought to know up to 100 words. Many are capable of learning 10 or more new words a day, assuming they hear new words in their environments (CDE 2009; Marotz & Allen 2012).

Expressive Language

Expressive language involves being able to communicate verbally or nonverbally (sign language or body language). Young children need both expressive and receptive language to develop literacy and math skills, which involve being able to recognize that words, numbers, signs, and symbols have meanings that can be understood and communicated to others.

The primary language for nonverbal children and those with few words is the cry. Infant cries become differentiated a few weeks after birth, which is about the earliest they might begin group care. Caregivers who know individual babies well recognize each child's expressions of hunger, boredom, pain, anger, tiredness, and fear from the sound of their cries. Taking cries seriously by responding as soon as possible, and doing so with kindness, gentle hands, and reassuring words, shows respect for babies as persons and as communication partners.

Infants start smiling socially around the second month, and together with characteristic vocalizations of cooing, gooing, and *ah-goo* sounds, they are ready and willing conversation partners. Caregivers should spend as much face-to-face time as possible with them, dancing back and forth to help establish the pattern and rhythms of human conversation. Sometime around 3 to 6 months, children start playing more with their vocalizations, making deep gurgling sounds, and razzing with their tongue and lips. These activities provide valuable exercise for the muscles needed for speech.

At 6 to 9 months, infants shift from cooing to babbling, which is the repetition of consonant sounds, such as *dadadada, mmamamaamam*, and *b-b-b-b*. After a couple of months of practice, children add short and long vowel sounds to the repeated consonants and can be heard babbling with inflections that sound very much like speech in another language (or like one of their parents or caregivers!). At the same time, they may start shaking their heads no or gesturing emphatically, clearly communicating when they do not want something, like more food or a diaper change.

Between about 9 and 12 months, single-word expressions emerge in reference to objects, people, or actions, such as "doggy," "bye-bye," and "oh-oh!" Caregivers will notice toddlers clearly trying to imitate words others say, along with the intonation. Toward the end of this period, two-word sentences emerge, usually consisting of a noun and a verb or a question or request—for example, "Go play," "More milk," and "Where Mommy?" Some of these short sentences convey great meaning, more than the child is able to verbalize just yet—for example, "Daddy go?" delivered with a look of intense worry on a tear-stained face.

After this point, expressive language usually takes off rapidly. By 12 to 18 months, many children can say seven to 20 words that adults can understand; by the second birthday, more than 50; and by age 3, adults can usually understand 200 to 300 words that children say.

Early Literacy and Mathematical Understanding

Acquisition of literacy and mathematical understanding is built upon the foundation of language acquisition. Understanding and using symbols for reading, writing, and mathematics requires practice, which is best done through symbolic play, where one object or thing represents (symbolizes) something else—a wooden block represents a cell phone, a wooden spoon becomes a magic wand. When children are read to frequently, they have favorite stories and can point to details in pictures books if asked. Starting at about 12 months, infants like to scribble and color using crayons and markers. Such experiences help them develop an understanding that what is being said is related to the symbols on the page.

Focus on Infants and Toddlers

Number sense is an understanding of how numbers work, a necessary skill for using numbers in everyday life and to solve problems. Caregivers can help young children acquire the receptive vocabulary and understanding of concepts related to number, quantity, speed, distance, size, and comparison, and build an understanding of them within their environments. Doing puzzles, sorting and classifying, and stacking and counting with infants and toddlers are fun ways to build number sense.

❖ ❖ ❖

The information in this chapter is provided to give caregivers in birth-to-3 settings a broad overview of concepts and topics in child development to help them in the important work they do. Each topic could be an entire book! It is important to continue to read, access resources, attend workshops, and take courses to expand your knowledge and thinking about the topics highlighted here and to stay current in the field of early childhood education.

Developmentally Appropriate Examples to Consider

The framework of developmentally appropriate practice derives from what the early childhood field knows from research and experience about how children develop and learn. Major points from this knowledge base are highlighted in the position statement and summarized in Chapter 3. Because no learning tool clarifies understanding better than examples, the chart below presents many more examples of infant/toddler practices to consider.

The chart addresses developmentally appropriate practice in six areas particularly important to infant/toddler care: relationships between caregiver and child, environment, exploration and play, routines, reciprocal relationships with families, and policies. The set of examples offered here is not exhaustive, and the goal is not to describe best practice comprehensively. We have tried to capture major aspects of practice that one sees in excellent early childhood programs and, by contrast, in those programs that in some respects have not achieved a high level of quality. Neither is the aim to issue a prescriptive formula to be rigidly followed. Instead, the examples are meant to encourage readers to reflect on their practice. Establishing a habit of thoughtful reflection is essential in caring for young children because of their varying family backgrounds, preferences, and needs.

In the chart's left column, under the heading "Developmentally Appropriate," are examples of practices consistent with available research and that most in the field agree promote young children's optimal learning and development. The examples in the "In Contrast" column are intended to aid reflection by helping readers see clearly the kinds of things that well-intentioned adults might do but that are not likely to serve children well. Many of the "In Contrast" examples are

This chapter was first published in *Developmentally Appropriate Practice in Early Childhood Programs Serving Children From Birth Through Age 8* (Copple & Bredekamp 2009).

very prevalent in early childhood settings. A few of those practices are dangerous or would cause children lasting damage. Others are unlikely to harm children significantly but also are less likely to promote their optimal development. Sometimes context affects whether a practice should be used or adapted.

Where they appear, the comments sections expand on the practice examples presented in the chart cells above them. Many of the comments speak of cultural factors to consider when determining what practices to use. The cultural dimension, important for any age group, is particularly significant with infants and toddlers. In their first three years of life, children are learning who they are and where they belong. Thus, the experiences that infants and toddlers have with their caregivers in the care setting need to be in harmony with what their family wants them to learn. Achieving harmony between program and home comes about through care that is respectful and responsive to each family's cultural preferences for their child, negotiated within the best practices framework.

Finally, most of the examples are phrased as descriptions of what caregivers do or fail to do. For the "In Contrast" examples, however, that wording is not meant to imply that deficient or questionable care is necessarily caregivers' fault. Most infant and toddler caregivers are working hard and doing their best—but often constrained by very challenging circumstances, including limited training, inadequate staff:child ratios, low compensation, high staff turnover, and meager resources. The hope of this chapter is to help them in their efforts.

Infants

Developmentally appropriate	In contrast

Relationship Between Caregiver and Child

Primary Caregiving, Continuity of Care

Developmentally appropriate	In contrast
There is sufficient continuity of care to ensure that every infant and parent can form a positive relationship with one or two primary caregivers.	○ Infants are shifted from group to group or cared for by whichever adult is available at the moment.
The infant's primary caregiver comes to know the child and family well, and so is able to respond to that child's individual temperament, needs, and cues and develop a mutually satisfying pattern of communication with the child and family.	○ Caregivers are not familiar with the preferences and cues of individual infants because they do not have the same children in their care consistently. ○ Caregivers do not see relating to families as part of their job; they may even view forming warm relationships with parents as unprofessional.
Infants and their parents are greeted warmly each morning by each child's primary caregiver, who is available to each infant upon arrival and helps the child become a part of the caregiver's small group of children as needed. A peaceful transition time for parent and child is a part of the daily routine.	○ Caregivers receive children hurriedly and without individual attention. Babies are promptly placed in a crib or infant seat with little or no caregiver interaction. ○ Caregivers receive children warmly but neglect to give any attention to the family member who brought the baby.

Developmentally appropriate	In contrast

Relationship Between Caregiver and Child (cont.)

Primary Caregiving, Continuity of Care (cont.)

Comments on primary caregiving and continuity of care:

—*Primary caregiving* means that each child is cared for by only the same one or two adults, allowing the adult to come to know the child very well and the child to form a strong emotional bond (*attachment*) with that adult. *Continuity of care* means a child stays with the same primary caregiver in the same peer group over many months (and from year to year, if possible). If caregivers change frequently, infants either never attach or must continually deal with separation and readjustment, which can make both infants and parents feel insecure.

—Some cultures prefer *group attachment,* where children come to see themselves as part of a group of people. In this arrangement, the infant may have multiple caregivers, but there is stability in these relationships.

—Responsive and consistent infant care depends not only on individual caregivers but also on the program in the form of policies that make it a priority (see **Policies**).

Interactions

Developmentally appropriate	In contrast
Caregivers spend most of the day holding or touching infants, in one-on-one interactions that are warm and caring. Caregivers stroke and pat infants and talk in a pleasant, calm voice, making frequent eye contact.	○ Caregivers leave infants for long periods in cribs, playpens, or seats. They follow "no-touch" policies, ignoring the importance of touch to children's healthy development. ○ Caregivers interact with infants harshly or impersonally, or they ignore infants' cues that they do not want to be held or touched. Or they give more attention and warmth to certain children (e.g., in family care, favoring their own child).
Caregivers learn and watch for each infant's cues, so they are able to judge when the baby needs to eat, is uncomfortable, or would like to be held. Every infant gets responsive care.	○ Caregivers give attention and care according to their own schedule or preferences rather than children's.
Caregivers respond consistently to infants' needs for food and comfort in ways that are *caring* and *specific* to each child. Over time infants develop trust in these adults who care for them, from which they generalize that the world is a secure place for them to explore and that they themselves are loveable and worthy.	○ Caregivers are unpredictable in their responses, don't respond at all, or respond in ways that are not caring or specific to the child.
Caregivers know that infants are curious about each other and are just beginning to build social skills. Because touching is a natural urge, caregivers allow interested infants to explore each other, while making sure that they treat each other gently.	○ Caregivers do not allow infants to touch each other, even gently. ○ Caregivers push infants to play together when they have no interest in doing so. If one child is very rough with another, adults take no action to protect the child who is being hurt.

Developmentally appropriate	In contrast

Relationship Between Caregiver and Child (cont.)

Interactions (cont.)

Caregivers respect infants' individual abilities and respond positively as each baby develops new abilities (i.e., they give children no more assistance than they need). Experiencing caregivers' pleasure in their achievements, infants feel competent and enjoy mastering new skills.

○ Infants are pushed to develop skills even though they demonstrate that they are not yet ready.

○ Caregivers do things for children that they could do for themselves or that they could do with some assistance.

Comments on interactions:

—There is much evidence that one-on-one interactions keep child and adult close both physically (e.g., touching, gazing) and emotionally (Honig 2002). At the same time, these kinds of interactions may not be valued in all cultures. For example, some cultures establish intimacy through eye contact, but others don't.

—Cultures that value verbal language closely attend to and encourage infants' beginning vocalizations. But in cultures where infants are in constant physical contact with a family member, interactions occur through body language, not words.

—To allow two infants to safely interact physically, caregivers often put them on the floor together. This can make families uncomfortable if they are from a culture where infants are carried constantly by a caregiver and so are rarely on the floor or close enough to play together.

—Wanting babies to feel good about themselves and their individual accomplishments can be regarded negatively as personal pride by cultures that value humility.

Respect for Infants as People

Caregivers often talk to the infant about what is going on (e.g., "I am putting your sweater on now so we can go outside"), especially to an older infant who can understand somewhat. Caregivers treat each baby like the person he or she is—that is, caregivers respect the child not just as "becoming" but as already "being" someone who has preferences, moods, and thoughts.

○ Caregivers move the infant about without explaining why, sometimes abruptly or at the adult's convenience. They act as if children are a bother or are cute, doll-like objects rather than people.

Caregivers have healthy, accepting attitudes about children's bodies and their bodily functions.

○ Caregivers talk or act in a way that implies to infants that they are not to touch their bodies and that bodily functions are disgusting.

Caregivers adjust to each infant's individual feeding and sleeping schedules. They respect each infant's food preferences and eating style.

○ Caregivers follow schedules that are rigid and based on their needs rather than children's.

Comments on respect for infants as people:

—Treating babies as objects to be manipulated and not respecting or talking to them about what is happening to them can undermine their sense of security and control. And when they don't understand and aren't involved in the action, they are less inclined to cooperate.

—Each infant is an individual with likes and dislikes. To start learning each infant's preferred foods and eating style, caregivers can ask the family.

Developmentally appropriate	In contrast

Relationship Between Caregiver and Child (cont.)

Communication

Recognizing that infants communicate through crying and body movements, caregivers respond to cries or calls of distress in ways that are calm, tender, and respectful.

○ Caregivers treat a crying child as a nuisance. Crying is ignored or responded to erratically at the convenience of the adult.

Caregivers observe and listen and respond to sounds the infant makes. Caregivers imitate children's vocalizations and appreciate the sounds as the beginnings of communication.

○ Caregivers are brusque and inattentive, ignoring the child's vocalizations.

○ Caregivers attend to the child's vocalizations, but they do not wait for the infants to finish before beginning to talk (i.e., adults don't wait their turn in the "conversation").

Caregivers frequently talk with, sing to, and read to infants. Even before babies understand speech, language is a vital, lively part of the communication that adults have with children; it is important in infants' language development, as well.

○ Caregivers use language indiscriminately, either too much or too little, and they use a very limited range of words in their conversations with infants.

Comments on communication:

—When crying babies get a response from their caregiver and their needs are met reasonably soon, the amount of crying diminishes. In cultures where a baby is continually carried by a caregiver, infants tend to cry less, because they communicate their needs in a different way.

Environment

Sensory Environment

The play areas offer children a variety of touch experiences (e.g., soft and hard areas, different levels).

○ There is no carpeting and no contrast between soft areas and harder ones. The play areas are sterile, designed for easy cleaning, but lack different textures or levels.

The visual environment has a good balance of things that are interesting to look at from the baby's perspective. It is uncluttered and aesthetically pleasing.

○ Walls are cluttered with posters and other items. The visually overwhelming environment creates a confusing blur for babies, makes it hard for them to focus on any one thing, and may even make them irritable.

○ Surroundings are sterile and bland.

Developmentally appropriate	In contrast

Environment (cont.)

Sensory Environment (cont.)

Caregivers have arranged and decorated the space from the perspective of babies lying on their backs.	○ No visual displays are in an infant's line of sight. Or the display makes babies uncomfortable (e.g., a bright overhead light) or overstimulated (e.g., books with bright colors along crib walls), and it can't be escaped. ○ Caregivers provide visual elements (e.g., mobile over a crib) with the aim of entertaining the baby as a substitute for appropriate social interaction with other babies and adults.
The environment is a mix of quiet and sounds. To judge what is just the right amount of sound, caregivers look for cues in babies' reactions. Caregivers play music and other recordings that infants enjoy.	○ Caregivers play music that they prefer, often loudly and constantly. Babies find the sound environment overstimulating or distracting (e.g., infants have difficulty focusing on speech sounds and hearing their own vocalizations).

Comments on sensory environment:

—Hard floors give babies the feedback and resistance they need to experience gravity and learn motor and sensory skills. Soft is nice, but when the whole environment is soft, infants have a harder time moving (e.g., rolling over, crawling).

—Although their vision is not as good as that of adults, infants have considerable visual abilities even at birth, and these improve substantially over the first few months of life. By 4 or 5 months of age, infants typically recognize familiar faces and easily distinguish shades of light and dark.

—Although a relatively quiet environment is ideal for most infants, those who come from homes filled with people, noise, and activity get used to what would be distressing to another child.

Play Spaces

Play areas are comfortable: They have surfaces that are both soft (e.g., carpeting) and hard (e.g., vinyl flooring). Comfortable furniture for adults is available for caregivers/parents and infants to relax in together.	○ There is no area where an adult can sit comfortably with an infant.
Areas are the right size for the age of the babies and the number in the group: Young infants have small and cozy areas, so they can feel secure. Older infants enjoy periods of both quiet play by themselves and play with other babies. They have ample space to move freely (e.g., roll over). Once they are mobile, they have space to roll or crawl toward interesting objects.	○ Spaces are too large and open, so infants feel insecure. ○ Spaces are cramped and/or unsafe for children who are learning how to move their bodies.

Developmentally appropriate	In contrast

Environment (cont.)

Play Spaces (cont.)

Open areas (indoor and outdoor) for mobile infants encourage them to test gross motor skills and coordination with balls, push and pull toys, wagons, and other big play equipment. There also are safe, right-sized climbing structures, ramps, and steps.

○ Caregivers allow balls and other moving toys outdoors only.

○ There are no structures for crawling up/down or under/through. Or structures are safe only for toddlers or older children.

Caregivers put infants in cribs mainly to sleep, not to play. During play periods, they place babies on firm surfaces where they can move freely and safely.

Caregivers move nonmobile infants periodically throughout the day to give them different perspectives and a reasonable variety in what children are able to look at and explore.

○ Babies are confined to cribs, infant seats, or playpens for long periods (e.g., for caregivers' convenience or "to keep infants safe").

○ Children are able to move around and explore, but caregivers don't separate nonmobile babies from mobile ones. Or they don't stay nearby to protect children from getting hurt.

Comments on play spaces:

—It's important that caregivers as well as children feel comfortable. Long days in a setting that doesn't support the adults' physical comfort will add to their fatigue and stress, which is bad for children.

—Being outdoors, rather than being inside all the time, contributes to children's health and well-being as well as giving them a larger variety of sensory experiences. Even in colder climates, infants benefit from being outside every day.

Exploration and Play

Playful Interactions

Caregivers value infants' exploration and play. They observe what each child is doing or focusing on, comment verbally on the play, and provide a safe environment for it. This quiet support encourages children's active engagement.

○ Infants are interrupted; toys are dangled, put into their hands, or whisked away. Caregivers impose their own ideas on the play without regard to the child's interests, or they even play with toys themselves while the child merely watches.

Caregivers play with babies in ways that are sensitive to each child's interests and tolerance for physical movements, loud sounds, or other changes to the child's surroundings.

○ Attempting to be playful, caregivers frighten, tease, or upset children with their unpredictable behaviors.

Developmentally appropriate	In contrast

Exploration and Play (cont.)

Playful Interactions (cont.)

Appropriate games, such as peekaboo, are played with interested infants, the adult being careful not to intrude on how the infant wants to play or interrupt the infant's concentration.

○ Games and activities are imposed on infants regardless of their interest.

○ Caregivers are rarely playful with babies.

Caregivers often hold infants on their laps to enjoy a book together. Much of this book time is shared page turning, commenting on pictures, and conversation around the content of the book.

○ Caregivers pressure babies to engage with books, expecting them to sit still and stay focused the way older children would.

Comments on playful interactions:

—A pattern of adult interruptions of infants' exploration and play contributes to short attention spans, so caregivers need to be sensitive to the baby's engagement and avoid breaking in.

—In some cultures, playing with babies is not encouraged. Babies spend their time in adult settings (e.g., carried in a sling during chores, brought into the family workplace). Playing may be something babies do on their own, not with adults. Caregivers may need to help adults from those cultures understand the benefits of play-oriented infant care.

—Some adults were not brought up around books; some are functionally illiterate. Rather than having a book culture in their homes, such families sometimes have an oral or storytelling tradition, which caregivers can encourage parents to share with their children and perhaps with the group as a whole. Caregivers can also lend books to families and encourage them to look at these with children and point out and talk about things on the pages.

Objects to Manipulate and Explore

Caregivers appreciate that very young babies play first with their own bodies as they explore what their major muscles can do, change positions, feel sensations, and eventually discover their own hands and feet.

○ Caregivers restrain babies (e.g., in infant seats, swings, restrictive clothing) or keep them in cribs to restrict their movements and exploration.

Caregivers provide play objects made of materials and scaled to a size that lets infants grasp, chew, and manipulate them (e.g., clutch balls, teethers, soft and washable dolls or play animals).

○ Caregivers provide toys too large to handle or so small that infants could choke on or swallow them. They hang toys above the nonmobile infant, making them available only to look at or perhaps bat at, but not to manipulate, mouth, or fully explore.

| Developmentally appropriate | In contrast |

Exploration and Play (cont.)

Objects to Manipulate and Explore (cont.)

Caregivers provide a variety of safe household items that infants can use as play materials (e.g., measuring cups, wooden spoons, unbreakable bowls).

○ Household items, which help make the care setting more homelike, are not provided.

Books made of sturdy cardboard (board books) are placed where babies can easily reach them. The books show everyday objects and activities; the people depicted are diverse (e.g., in age, abilities, ethnicity, culture, family configuration).

○ Books are not provided (because "babies can't read" or "they'll just get ruined").

○ The books available are made of paper that tears easily. Books do not show images of things familiar or interesting to children.

Once babies can reach and grasp, caregivers provide play objects carefully chosen to be responsive to the child's actions and perhaps allowing different types of manipulation (e.g., turning, squeezing, inserting).

○ Caregivers provide toys that are battery powered or windup, so the baby just watches. Toys lack variety in texture, size, and shape. Caregivers put toys into the infant's hand before the grasp reflex weakens, so the child can't let go of them.

Any play objects that make noise are made so the infant can see and understand where the noise comes from.

○ Rattles and other noise-making and busy-box toys have hidden mechanisms, so any explorations don't help the baby understand how the object works.

Comments on objects to manipulate and explore:

—Babies get an early sense of power when they discover what they can do with their bodies. Accidental at first, then growing more purposeful as babies develop, experiencing their own movement teaches babies they can make things happen. Practice and repetition of self-chosen movements support self-regulation.

—In some cultures, play objects are less important, especially if infants are in body contact most or all of the time with their caregivers. Sensory experiences (i.e., sights, sounds), rather than objects, are what such infants "play" with. Families from such cultures may stress their baby developing observation skills more than manipulation skills.

Organization and Access to Materials

Play materials are well organized and made accessible to children. For example, caregivers organize objects for different activities on different shelves (e.g., fill-and-empty materials are on a shelf separate from three-piece puzzles or moving/pushing toys).

○ Caregivers give no thought to organization. They are unaware that how they arrange toys and materials can affect how children interact with the items.

Developmentally appropriate	In contrast

Exploration and Play (cont.)

Organization and Access to Materials (cont.)

Play materials are stored on open shelves at children's eye level and within their reach. Caregivers space individual items so infants can make deliberate choices. Infants with special needs who are developmentally ready and able to manipulate objects (but may be challenged in mobility skills) have access to play objects.

○ Toys are dumped in a box and come out in a jumble. Caregivers don't understand that choosing from a jumble isn't the same to a child as being able to look at an orderly selection and make a careful choice.

○ Toys are kept out of children's reach. Caregivers make the child ask for a desired toy, or they make the selection for the child.

Comments on organization and access to materials:

—Some cultures emphasize human relationships above manipulating objects; in such families, adults may remove a toy or other object if it is distracting the infant from focusing on a person or people. And, while many cultural groups in the United States (and other Western countries) stress independence, families from a culture that places greater value on interdependence, who want their children to have very close, enduring connections with the family, may resist their child becoming more self-sufficient as an infant.

Routines

Caregivers are attentive to infants during caregiving routines such as eating, sleeping, diapering, changing clothes, and the like. The caregiver explains what is happening and involves the infant in the routine.

○ Routines are accomplished quickly and mechanically, without involving the infant. Little or no warm interaction takes place during routines.

Comments on routines:

—During routines, caregivers need to understand and follow good practice for health, safety, nutrition, and so on. For more specific information, please reference the NAEYC Health and Safety accreditation criteria: "Physical Environment" and "Health."

Eating

Infants feeding from a bottle are always held, their bodies at an angle. The primary caregiver or other familiar adult always feeds the infant.

○ Young infants are strapped into infant seats to be fed. Who holds the bottle is random, not the primary caregiver or even necessarily the same caregiver each time.

○ Babies are put into their infant seats or cribs and their bottles are propped up (e.g., on a pillow) while caregivers do other things.

Developmentally appropriate	In contrast

Routines (cont.)

Eating (cont.)

Developmentally appropriate	In contrast
Until infants can get into a sitting position on their own, they are placed in secure chairs such as highchairs (but only at mealtimes) or held by their primary caregiver or other familiar adult while being fed.	○ Babies are fed in highchairs, as a group, and not necessarily by the primary caregiver or even a familiar adult. ○ Highchairs are used to contain babies at other times during the day, too.
Caregivers use mealtimes as occasions for fostering children's independence and self-help mastery (e.g., letting mobile infants get into chairs by themselves, if they can). At the same time, caregivers try to accommodate a family's cultural preferences, which in some cases may include continuing to feed older infants.	○ Caregivers feed all children in the same way regardless of family preference.
Older infants eat in small groups at low tables. Their caregiver sits nearby to provide assistance as needed.	○ There are no small tables and chairs/stools to invite mobile infants to use their fine and gross motor control at mealtimes. ○ Large groups of children are fed in sequence or left to their own devices.
Caregivers allow children to feed themselves (including using utensils and cups), even when their efforts are messy. Finger foods are provided to increase children's likelihood of success.	○ Caregivers insist on feeding infants because it's more convenient or efficient (e.g., "she takes too long," "he always makes a mess"). ○ Caregivers expect infants to handle utensils or finger food neatly when children don't have those fine motor skills yet.
Small servings of healthy foods are offered, and each child selects how much to eat and when to stop. Mealtime is treated as a sociable, happy time.	○ Caregivers are not responsive to children's cues as to what foods they prefer and when they've had enough. Conversation between adults and children is limited. ○ Food is used to pacify or reward, or it is withheld as punishment.

Comments on eating:

—Eating meets a basic physical need; it also is a rich sensory and emotional experience.

—There are many different cultural perspectives on what, when, and how infants should eat. For example, talking while eating is not a universal practice, nor is eating with the fingers. In some cultures, spoon feeding children after they are capable of feeding themselves is regarded as a way of cementing a close bond between infant and adult.

Developmentally appropriate	In contrast

Routines (cont.)

Sleeping

The infant sleeping area is separate from active play and eating areas. Babies sleep in cribs reserved for them. Family members bring comforting objects from home to personalize their baby's crib.

○ Cribs line the walls in the play area. Cribs are all alike, and a baby is put into whichever crib is available. Infants do not have their own supplies, and there is nothing personal to help the baby feel that "this is my place."

The lighting is dim, but every infant is still visible. The sleeping area is quiet, perhaps with soft music while babies are falling asleep.

○ Bright lights and the sounds of playing babies or loud music disturb babies trying to sleep.

Each infant is put down by the primary caregiver or another familiar adult.

○ Different caregivers put babies down each time.

Comments on sleeping:

—That infants feel "at home" as much as possible is important in all caregiving activities, but especially for sleeping. For example, a baby whose large family lives in a small apartment where there is always activity and noise may have problems going to sleep in dim light, separate and apart from the activity of others.

Diapering

Infants are usually diapered by the child's primary caregiver or another familiar adult. Treated as a personal, one-on-one interaction—where the caregiver seeks the baby's attention and cooperation—diapering builds a sense of teamwork, and their relationship grows as a result.

○ One person diapers all babies, not necessarily the primary caregiver or an adult familiar to every child.

Diapering supplies and extra clothes for each child are within easy reach of the changing table. The caregiver has the needed time and tools to make diapering an efficient and pleasant experience for adult and child.

○ Because the diapering area is not well designed or organized, diapering takes a long time and can be uncomfortable and annoying to caregiver and infant alike.

○ In the rush to get diapers changed, the adult may forget or skip essential health and safety steps or handle the infant brusquely.

Developmentally appropriate	In contrast

Reciprocal Relationships With Families

Caregivers communicate daily with parents in a warm, honest, and respectful way to build mutual understanding and trust, which help in resolving any issues that may arise.	○ Caregivers communicate with parents rarely or only when there are problems or conflicts.
Caregivers help parents feel good about their babies (e.g., by sharing some of the positive and interesting things that happened that day).	○ Caregivers don't share the experiences they have with the child each day, causing parents to feel isolated from this part of their child's life. Or caregivers share plenty but focus on their negative experiences with the child instead of the positive.
Caregivers listen carefully to what parents say; they seek to understand parents' goals, priorities, and preferences for their children.	○ Rather than listening and trying to understand (the key to culturally responsive care particularly and family-responsive care more generally), caregivers do all or most of the talking. Caregivers may view their own cultural or other perspective as the only right one.
Caregivers support parents as being their child's most important relationship and as being ultimately responsible for the child's well-being and care (e.g., caregivers keep records of diaperings to share with parents). Caregivers focus on parents' expertise, attachment to their infants, and children's strong connections to their parents.	○ Caregivers set themselves up as experts, criticize parents' skills, or try to compete for babies' affection.
Caregivers and families collaborate in making decisions about how best to support children's development or handle issues if they do arise. Caregivers and parents figure out together how to solve problems and see beyond differences to common concerns.	○ Caregivers avoid difficult issues or make decisions unilaterally rather than problem solving with parents. ○ Caregivers see parents as the "problem" rather than part of the solution.
Caregivers are respectful of parents' cultural and family preferences. Using a team approach, caregivers try to accommodate those preferences, if it can be done in a developmentally appropriate way, and, if it cannot, try to help parents understand why (e.g., parents want caregivers to leave the baby alone to cry himself out whenever he cries).	○ Caregivers ignore or disparage parents' goals or preferences for their children. Caregivers may see their opinions as superior or view preferences other than their own as being odd or wrong rather than just different. ○ Caregivers capitulate to parent demands (e.g., spanking) or preferences, even when these are at odds with developmentally appropriate practice.

Developmentally appropriate	In contrast

Reciprocal Relationships With Families (cont.)

Caregivers always make parents feel welcome (e.g., warmly receive and support nursing mothers who are able to come in for breastfeeding).

○ Caregivers communicate a competitive or patronizing attitude to parents, or they make parents feel like they are in the way.

Pictures of infants and their family members are hung on walls where infants can see them.

○ Caregivers try not to remind infants of their families because they hope to avoid any displays of separation anxiety.

○ Decorations are at adult eye level and do not include family photos.

Comments on reciprocal relationships with families:

—Helping parents feel good about their child's positive qualities leads to family support for those qualities. Most parents want to feel good about their child, but in some cultures they may not want to hear that their child feels good about him- or herself. In cultures that value humility over self-pride, adults may want to downplay a child's positive qualities, fearing the child will get conceited.

—Sometimes family preferences can be accommodated; other times caregivers see the parents' request as one they cannot go along with. Then a conversation between caregivers and family about their different perspectives is called for.

—Seeing images of family members reminds infants of their loved ones and helps them feel that they belong to their family and their family is connected to the program. If seeing the images upsets infants, coping with feelings is one of the early lessons they can learn in programs where the caregivers are willing to help them with separation.

Policies

Health and Safety

Caregivers follow health and safety procedures, including proper hand washing methods and universal precautions to limit the spread of infectious disease.

There are clearly written sanitation procedures specific to each task or routine to help staff remember to follow procedures completely and consistently.

○ Policies and procedures to ensure a sanitary facility have not been clearly thought through and are not written down. Consequently, adults forget hand washing or other essential steps in diapering, cleaning cribs and play areas, handling food, and cleaning food-preparation areas. Caregivers are not consistent in maintaining sanitary conditions and procedures.

Developmentally appropriate	In contrast

Policies (cont.)

Health and Safety (cont.)

The space has been constructed and set up with health and safety in mind (e.g., walls are painted with lead-free, easy-to-clean paint; carpeting and flooring are easy to clean; diapering and food-preparation areas are separate; storage for disinfectants, gloves, and plastic bags is clearly labeled).

○ The space is not organized to foster health and safety (e.g., supplies, even disinfectants, do not have a designated space out of the reach of infants, so caregivers tend to leave them on the diapering counter).

○ The environment is clean and safe but has a sterile, institutional feel.

Infants are placed on their backs for sleeping unless otherwise directed by a doctor.

○ Caregivers place children to sleep in any position that seems to make children happy or to quiet them down quickest.

Comments on health and safety:

—Caregivers need training, support, and reminders to understand and consistently follow proper health and safety procedures (e.g., to diaper hygienically). For more specific information, please reference the NAEYC Health and Safety accreditation criteria: "Physical Environment" and "Health."

Staffing

Program hires caregivers who enjoy working with infants in particular and who have had training specifically related to infant development and caregiving. Caregivers are open to ongoing training and support in order to deepen their understanding and skills in caring for this age group.

○ Program hires caregivers who view working with infants as a custodial chore or who have little or no training specific to infant development and caregiving.

Caregivers cope well with stress, and they model in their interactions with others (e.g., coworkers, family members, directors) the style and tone they want children to develop.

○ Caregivers don't cope well under stress; they become tearful, aggressive, or overwrought. Or caregivers are cold and aloof and never show any emotion.

Program limits group size and the adult:child ratio to allow caregivers one-on-one interactions with and intimate knowledge of individual babies.

○ Groups are too large and staff:child ratio too high to permit individual attention and constant supervision.

In its staffing patterns, the program is committed to primary caregiving.

○ Staffing patterns require infants to relate to more than two adults during the caregiving day.

Developmentally appropriate	In contrast

Policies (cont.)

Staffing (cont.)

In its staffing patterns, the program ensures continuity of care. Child and caregiver are able to maintain their relationship, and each child's ongoing relationship with the other children in the group is supported.

○ Staffing patterns shift caregivers around from infant to infant or group to group. This may even be intentional (e.g., so "children don't get too attached").

○ Child groupings change constantly (e.g., daily to suit the schedule preferences of staff, or periodically as infants are "graduated" to the next room and new caregivers).

○ High staff turnover (e.g., due to inadequate compensation, poor working conditions) results in low continuity and frequent disruption of infants' budding attachments to caregivers.

Comments on staffing:

—No one automatically has the knowledge of how to care for infants in groups, and not all adults have the interest in or disposition for infant care. When hiring and assigning staff, directors should consider individuals' strengths and preferences to determine the age group(s) with which each person fits best. Ability to work with other adults, attitudes toward diversity, and willingness to communicate about differences should also be considered. For more specific information, please reference the NAEYC Health and Safety accreditation criteria: "Teachers."

Toddlers

Relationship Between Caregiver and Child

Primary Caregiving, Continuity of Care

There is sufficient continuity of care to ensure that every toddler and parent can form a positive relationship with one or two primary caregivers.

○ Toddlers are shifted from group to group or cared for by whichever adult is available at the moment.

The toddler's primary caregiver comes to know the child and family well and so is able to respond to that child's individual temperament, needs, and cues and develop a mutually satisfying pattern of communication with the child and family.

○ Caregivers are not familiar with the preferences and cues of individual toddlers because they do not have the same children in their care consistently.

○ Caregivers do not see relating to families as part of their job; they may even view forming warm relationships with parents as unprofessional.

Developmentally appropriate	In contrast

Relationship Between Caregiver and Child (cont.)

Primary Caregiving, Continuity of Care (cont.)

Toddlers and their parents are greeted warmly by name by that child's primary caregiver when they arrive. Caregivers create smooth transitions by being available to the toddler who needs help with separating from parents, and by assisting each toddler in settling into the group by showing what has been set up and interacting with the child as needed.

○ Caregivers receive children hurriedly and without individual attention. Toddlers are expected to begin the day with free play and little adult interaction.

○ Caregivers receive toddlers warmly but neglect to give any attention to the family member who brought the child.

Comments on primary caregiving and continuity of care:

—*Primary caregiving* means that each child is cared for by only the same one or two adults, allowing the caregiver to come to know the child very well and the child to form a strong emotional bond (*attachment*) to that caregiver. *Continuity of care* means a child stays with the same primary caregiver in the same peer group over many months (and from year to year if possible). If caregivers change frequently, toddlers either never attach or must continually deal with separation and readjustment, which can make both toddlers and parents feel insecure.

—Some cultures prefer *group attachment,* where children come to see themselves as part of a group of people. In this arrangement, the toddler may have multiple caregivers, but there is stability in these relationships.

—Responsive and consistent toddler care depends not only on individual caregivers but also on the program in the form of policies that make it a priority (see **Policies**).

Interactions

Caregivers spend most of the day in one-on-one interactions with toddlers. The tone of the interactions is warm and caring; caregivers use pleasant, calm voices as well as simple language and nonverbal cues.

○ Caregivers leave some toddlers alone for long periods and give their energy and attention to other children (e.g., in family care, favoring their own child). Or caregivers focus their attention elsewhere altogether and don't interact much with children.

○ Caregivers interact with toddlers in a harsh or impersonal manner.

Caregivers learn each toddler's cues and respond consistently in ways that are *caring* and *specific* to each child, which lets the child explore, knowing he can trust the adults to be there for help or comfort as needed.

○ Caregivers give attention and care according to their own schedule or preferences rather than children's.

○ Caregivers are unpredictable in their responses, don't respond at all, or respond in ways that are not caring or specific to the child.

Developmentally appropriate	In contrast

Relationship Between Caregiver and Child (cont.)

Interactions (cont.)

Caregivers frequently read to toddlers—to one child individually or to groups of two or three—always in close physical contact. Caregivers sing with toddlers, do finger plays, and act out simple stories or folktales, with children participating actively.

○ Caregivers impose "group time" on toddlers, expecting a large group to listen or watch an activity without children having opportunities to participate or to interact with caregivers individually.

Caregivers comfort toddlers and let them know they are valued through warm responsive touches, such as pats on the back and hugs and holding toddlers in their laps. Caregivers are sensitive to whether a child welcomes the touches.

○ Caregivers follow "no-touch" policies, ignoring the importance of touch to children's healthy development.

○ Caregivers ignore children's cues that they do not want to be held or touched.

Caregivers create an emotionally and physically inclusive classroom. They give every toddler warm, responsive care. They make sure that spatial organization, materials, and activities are planned such that all children can participate actively (e.g., a child with a physical disability eats at the table with other children).

○ Caregivers do not include children with special needs in all activities (e.g., a child who requires adaptive equipment or special procedures eats or plays apart from peers).

To satisfy toddlers' natural curiosity, caregivers give simple, brief, accurate responses when children stare at or ask questions about a person with a disability or other difference.

○ Caregivers disregard children's curiosity about a person's disability or adaptive equipment.

○ Caregivers criticize a child for noticing or asking questions about differences.

○ Caregivers make comments or offer explanations that show their own discomfort or disparage others with disabilities.

Comments about interactions:

—There is much evidence that one-on-one interactions keep child and adult close physically and emotionally (Honig 2002). Touch is a mode of communication that is particularly important in the early years. Some toddlers shy away from touches, and caregivers need to be sensitive to individual differences. Where and how a person may be touched also is highly cultural; in some cultures being touched on the head is considered demeaning or even dangerous.

—In some cultures, children—even toddlers—are expected to learn by observing rather than by participating (e.g., sitting for a long time in a large group). Toddlers generally are or like to be physically active, however. In the early childhood setting, they should be allowed to move around and participate in play and active learning throughout most of the day.

—Caregivers must make the effort to integrate children with special needs as fully as possible. After giving curious toddlers a simple explanation of the disability or difference, the adult might say a bit about the child's interests and abilities ("Susan likes to draw and finger-paint. Here's a picture she made this morning").

Developmentally appropriate	In contrast

Relationship Between Caregiver and Child (cont.)

Respect for Toddlers as People

Caregivers have appropriate expectations for toddlers. When a child is trying to do something (e.g., putting on her boots), the caregiver watches to see what the toddler can manage on her own and provides support as needed.

○ Caregivers are impatient with toddlers who are learning new skills. Because it is faster, the adult does tasks for toddlers that they could have done themselves.

○ Caregivers foster overdependence; children are overprotected and made to feel inadequate.

○ Caregivers often allow toddlers to become frustrated, to the extent that children become very upset or give up on tasks they cannot do or problems they can't solve alone.

Caregivers have healthy, accepting attitudes about children's bodies and their bodily functions.

○ Caregivers talk or act in a way that makes toddlers feel ashamed of their bodies and think bodily functions are disgusting.

Caregivers respect each child's developing preferences for familiar objects, foods, and people. They permit toddlers to keep their own favorite objects, and they let children choose (from a limited set of options) what they prefer to eat or wear.

○ Caregivers prohibit toddlers from bringing a favored object (e.g., a blanket or toy) from home. Or they arbitrarily take the object away or expect a toddler to share it with other children.

○ Children are not given choices, and having/expressing preferences is not encouraged. Children are all expected to do the same thing.

Caregivers respect toddlers' interest in objects—to carry objects around with them, collect objects, move them from one place to another, and to roam around or sit and parallel play with toys and other objects.

○ Caregivers restrict objects to certain locations ("Books must stay in the reading corner"); they do not tolerate children's hoarding, collecting, or carrying objects about.

Comments on respect for toddlers as people:

—Toddlers are developing confidence in their abilities, which leads to increased self-esteem. Some cultures downplay self-pride and teach humility instead, and families may raise issues relating to this difference with caregivers.

—When a family's culture gives greater priority to *inter*dependence than to independence, caregivers may view some parent behaviors as being overprotective or creating an overly dependent child when the actual goal is mutual dependence. At times, these parents may emphasize teaching the child to graciously receive help when he is trying to do something on his own.

—Toddlers' awareness of themselves as individuals who have preferences and personal possessions is growing; allowing them to practice making choices is good for their self-concept. Children at this age begin developing a notion of having "favorites," which their caregivers should recognize and respect. Children find comfort in familiar objects and also enjoy figuring out which objects belong to categories or groups.

Developmentally Appropriate Examples to Consider

Developmentally appropriate	In contrast

Relationship Between Caregiver and Child (cont.)

Communication

An adult initiating a conversation with a toddler gives the child ample time to respond. Caregivers also listen attentively for children's verbal initiations and respond to these.

○ Caregivers talk *at* toddlers and do not wait for a response.
○ Adult voices dominate. Or caregivers do not speak to children because they think they are too young to converse.

Caregivers label or name objects, describe events, and reflect feelings ("You're angry that Yvette took the block?") to help children learn new words. Caregivers simplify their language for toddlers who are just beginning to talk. Then as children acquire their own words, caregivers expand on the toddler's language (Child: "Mark sock." Adult: "Oh, that's Mark's missing sock, and you found it").

○ Caregivers do not try to build toddlers' understanding of the world around them through interacting with them. They assume toddlers are too young for any level of verbal communication.
○ Caregivers either talk "baby talk" or use language that is too complex for toddlers to understand.

Caregivers ask the family what sounds, words, and nonverbal cues their toddler uses to better understand what the child means when she uses beginning speech or a home language that is not understood by the caregivers.

○ Caregivers do not talk with parents about the toddler's speech, communication patterns, or home language. They cannot understand what the toddler is trying to convey, which frustrates the child in her efforts to communicate.
○ Caregivers tell parents to speak English to their children even if the parents lack facility in the English language.

Caregivers learn what each child's cries mean (e.g., fear, frustration, sleepiness, pain) and when to wait (e.g., to see if the child solves his own problem) or take action. They respond promptly to toddlers' cries or other signs of distress.

○ Crying is ignored or responded to erratically or at the caregiver's convenience.

Comments on communication:

—Talking *with* toddlers instead of *at* them greatly facilitates their language development and expands their vocabulary, which in turn eventually will help them learn to read. Language use can vary greatly from culture to culture. For example, in some cultures, children are never asked questions to which the adult already knows the answer. So a child from such a family may think it strange behavior and not respond if the caregiver holds up a book and asks, "What is this?"

—It's very important to learn from parents how their toddlers express themselves at home. Understanding the context behind what the toddler is trying to convey, which parents can often provide, facilitates communication and builds relationships. When the toddler's home language is different from the program's, every effort should be made to support the child's continued language development in both. Speaking one's family language is a part of identity formation and connection with the home culture.

—Although words will eventually replace it, crying is a form of toddler communication, so caregivers should seek to understand what a child is crying about, rather than just trying to make it stop or ignoring it.

Developmentally appropriate	In contrast

Relationship Between Caregiver and Child (cont.)

Positive Guidance

In their interactions with others, caregivers model how they want children to behave. To help a toddler resolve differences, caregivers use words to express what is happening and what the toddler might be feeling ("You want to play with that car? Shantel is playing with it now; let's see if we can find another car on the shelf").

○ Caregivers themselves show aggression, shout, or exhibit a lack of coping behaviors under stress.

○ Caregivers' attempts to punish or control an aggressive toddler escalate the hostility. They do not model for toddlers the words to say to resolve a conflict.

Caregivers patiently redirect toddlers to help guide them toward controlling their own impulses and behavior.

○ Caregivers do not anticipate behaviors that are likely to occur and so do not prevent children from getting hurt or hurting others.

○ Caregivers ignore disputes and other problematic behaviors, leading to a chaotic atmosphere.

○ Caregivers punish infractions harshly, frightening and humiliating children.

Caregivers recognize that toddlers constantly test limits and express opposition ("No!") as part of developing a healthy sense of self as an autonomous individual.

○ Caregivers punish children for asserting themselves or for saying no.

Caregivers try to limit telling children no only to situations that relate to their immediate safety or emotional well-being. Adults give positively worded directions or choices ("Bang on the drum or the floor"), not just restrictions ("Don't bang on the table").

○ Caregivers are constantly telling toddlers no without giving an alternative. Or they become involved in power struggles over issues that do not relate to the child's safety or well-being.

Comments on positive guidance:

—Understanding how toddler behaviors relate to their stage of development helps caregivers to respond in positive ways without taking children's negativity personally or getting upset and angry. Staying out of power struggles is particularly important.

—Observation is an important skill for caregivers to develop so they are able to anticipate toddlers' actions and prevent dangerous or aggressive situations. Toddlers need to know that the adult will provide control when they lack it.

—Adults' responses to a toddler's behavior play a role in forming that child's sense of self. Because the value placed on a character trait such as cooperation or independence can vary by culture, caregivers and families may disagree about which behaviors are acceptable in their children. For example, if parents value obedience, they are less likely to want the caregiver to tolerate their toddler's testing limits and expressing opposition.

Developmentally appropriate	In contrast

Environment

Sensory Environment

Carpeting and flooring materials are selected to provide a soft background so that toddlers' eyes are drawn to the materials and activity choices.

○ Walls are cluttered. Or walls are sterile and bland.

○ Carpet and rugs are a confusion of distracting colors and patterns.

Toddlers' artwork and other creative projects are hung at a level just above their reach but low enough to be seen clearly. Caregivers display pictures of the children and their families or place them in albums for children to look at when they wish.

○ Toddlers' art is not displayed, or it is hung too high for them to see.

○ There is no indication of family involvement (e.g., no familiar objects from home).

Toddlers are surrounded by sensory objects for their play activities (e.g., banging objects, mounding sand, kneading dough). To a reasonable extent, they also can enjoy sensory play during routines such as hand washing (e.g., squirting the soap).

○ Children are denied the natural enjoyment of sensory play and exploring their environment during activities because "it's too noisy" or "messy" or "dirty." As a result, they play during cleanup or with their food whenever they can, often disrupting routines or requiring guidance.

Comments on sensory environment:

—When children with special needs are part of the program, caregivers need to make appropriate accommodations: For example, visually impaired children may need more contrast than usual (e.g., dark objects placed on a white tray) in order to focus on something. It also is vital that the arrangement of the environment remain much the same, so such children can find their way around. Constantly rearranging furniture and materials makes it very hard for a toddler with a visual impairment to concentrate on learning.

—Photos of home or family help toddlers deal with separation and feel that they belong to their family and the family is connected to the program. Not all cultures are comfortable with displays of home photographs, however; such a family may prefer to have an object from the home available for their child to see during the day.

—Toddlers learn about the world through exploration, which adults should encourage. As toddlers develop the ability to understand limits, caregivers can offer a larger variety of sensory materials.

Play and Learning Areas

Floor coverings are appropriate for the activities that occur there (e.g., easy-to-clean, shock-absorbent tiles for open areas where toddlers push and pull toys around and for art, eating, and water or sand play areas; low-pile, easy-to-clean carpeting or nonslip area rugs for quiet play areas).

○ Floors are covered with thick-pile carpeting that requires constant cleaning or is left dirty. Or the floor covering is hard and cold.

Developmentally appropriate	In contrast

Environment (cont.)

Play and Learning Areas (cont.)

Caregivers organize the space into interest or activity areas, including areas for concentrated small-group play, solitary play, dramatic play, and construction.	○ The space is not separated into interest areas, which makes it more difficult for children to get engaged in an activity.
Activity areas are separated by low partitions, shelves, or sitting benches, creating clear traffic patterns and making it less likely that running toddlers will inadvertently bump into and thus disturb peers engaged in concentrated play.	○ Space is open, with no clear traffic pattern from one interest area to another. Running toddlers bump into those who are engaged in concentrated play.
The environment contains private spaces, with room for one or two children. The spaces are situated to be easily supervised by adults.	○ The environment provides no private spaces. Or spaces are too private because they are out of view of adults.
Indoor areas are open and safe; space is set up to allow active, large muscle play.	○ Toddlers' indoor space is cramped and unsafe for children who are just learning how to move their bodies and need to run more than walk.
Toddlers' outdoor play space is separate from that of older children. Outdoor play equipment includes small-scale climbing equipment that lets toddlers go around and in and out, as well as solitary play equipment that requires supervision, such as swings and low slides. The equipment is sized so toddlers don't need to be lifted onto it or helped to get down.	○ Toddlers share outdoor space and equipment with larger, older children. Equipment is not designed for younger children; it is too large or difficult for toddlers to maneuver around in.

Comments on play and learning areas:

—How children behave in their environment depends to some extent on how the space is organized and the messages the room arrangement conveys. When there is a clear path from one interest area to another, the message is "Come see what else there is to do."

—Keeping program goals in mind is important when considering location of the various learning and caregiving areas. For example, placing the art area and the eating area close to a sink invites toddlers (with adult encouragement) to learn to use the sink on their own before and after these activities.

—Toddlers who spend long hours in group care need to be able to occasionally get away by themselves or perhaps with one other child. The value of spaces to provide privacy will be understood by parents who value independence. In some cultures, however, children are always part of the adult environment, and adults may be puzzled by spaces set up specifically for children.

Developmentally appropriate	In contrast

Exploration and Play

Play Development

Caregivers do everything they can to support toddlers' play so that children stay interested in an object or activity for increasing periods of time. For example, they don't interrupt when children are engaged, whether as individuals or as a group.

○ Because caregivers do not understand the importance of supporting children's play, they control or intrude on the play.

Caregivers respect toddlers' solitary and parallel play. When a toy is a favorite with children, adults provide a number of them to allow several toddlers to play with the toy at once.

○ Because caregivers do not understand the value of solitary and parallel play, they strive to get children to play together.

○ Adults expect toddlers to share. Popular toys are not provided in duplicate and are fought over constantly, while other toys are seldom used.

Caregivers play with toddlers, especially when they can help children to see expanded play possibilities. For example, some children may need adult help to play imaginatively, and caregivers can model for them (e.g., playing "tea party").

○ Caregivers never play with toddlers because the adults feel self-conscious or awkward.

Caregivers allow toddlers the freedom to explore their movements by testing what their bodies are capable of doing.

○ Caregivers spend time attempting to control toddlers' movements.

Caregivers understand that toddlers learn about the world through exploration and give them daily opportunities for exploratory activity at children's developmental level.

○ Caregivers do not offer exploratory play, or they limit it when it naturally occurs. They do not offer older, capable toddlers paint, sand, playdough, or clay because these materials are messy and require supervision.

Comments on play development:

—Some cultures do not view play as a tool for learning and development, and families from these cultures may not understand or appreciate the value of play. Caregivers must make clear why play is developmentally appropriate and important for toddlers.

—Toddlers need plenty of room to move. Encouraging their freedom of movement allows toddlers to learn about themselves, their world, and their own abilities and limitations; such learning helps them to avoid mishaps.

Developmentally appropriate	In contrast

Exploration and Play (cont.)

Objects to Manipulate and Explore

Toddlers are given appropriate art materials, such as large crayons, watercolor markers, and large pieces of paper. Caregivers offer nontoxic materials but avoid using food for art; toddlers are developing self-regulatory skills and must learn to distinguish between food and objects that are not to be eaten.	○ Because toddlers are likely to put things in their mouths, adults give them edible, often tasty finger paints or playdough.
Caregivers allow toddlers to explore and manipulate art materials and do not expect them to produce a finished art product.	○ Toddlers are "helped" by teachers to produce a product, copy the adult-made model, follow directions, or color a coloring book or sheets with adult drawings outlined.
Cups, paint cans, and other containers are small so that toddlers can easily manage them and cleanup is easy.	○ Toddlers must start and end art projects at the same time so that caregivers can get them ready and clean them up as a group.
A child-size sink with a good supply of paper towels is located near areas designated for messy activities so toddlers learn that cleaning up and washing their hands follow any messy activity.	○ Caregivers restrict messy activities. ○ Toddlers are not taught individual responsibility in cleaning up.
Sturdy picture books are provided. People of different ages, racial and cultural groups, family types, occupations, and abilities/disabilities are depicted.	○ Books are not available because they get might be torn or soiled. ○ Books do not contain objects familiar or interesting to children.

Comments on objects to manipulate and explore:

—Art gives toddlers opportunities to explore what various materials can do. They are just discovering what it feels like to put marks on paper or to play with paint or clay, and only later do they begin to pay attention to the result. Exploration is not about "making something" but rather about creating and observing some kind of effect. Not all toddlers like messy activities, however, and they shouldn't be pressured if they are reluctant. Most will eventually join in when they see their peers enjoying the activity.

—While excellent for older toddlers' explorations, paint, sand, playdough, and clay tend to be too advanced for young toddlers (16–18 months). If such materials were made available to young toddlers, caregivers would have to restrict and supervise play very closely to keep children safe.

—In some families, books are not part of either children's or adults' lives. If these families are carrying on oral instead of literary traditions, caregivers acknowledge and honor them by inviting storytelling into the program.

Developmentally Appropriate Examples to Consider

Developmentally appropriate	In contrast

Exploration and Play (cont.)

Organization and Access to Materials

Play materials are well organized. For example, caregivers organize objects for different activities on different shelves (e.g., fill-and-empty materials are on a shelf separate from three-piece puzzles or moving/pushing toys).

○ Caregivers give no thought to organization. They are unaware that how they arrange toys and materials can affect how children interact with the items.

Play materials are stored on open shelves at children's eye level and within their reach. For example, smocks are on low hooks so toddlers can reach them.

Toddlers with special needs who are developmentally ready and able to manipulate objects (but may be challenged in mobility skills) have access to play objects.

○ Toys are dumped in a box at the end of each day and come out in a jumble, making children dig through to choose something to play with.

○ Materials are inaccessible. Or they are too unwieldy for children to access on their own.

Caregivers space individual items so toddlers can make deliberate choices.

○ Caregivers don't understand that choosing from a jumble isn't the same to a toddler as being able to look at an orderly selection and make a careful choice.

○ Toys are kept out of children's reach. Caregivers make the toddler ask for the toy he wants, or they make the selection for him.

Comments on organization and access to materials:

—Some cultures emphasize human relationships above manipulating objects; such a family may want caregivers to remove a toy or other object if it is distracting the toddler from focusing on a person or people.

—Many cultures stress independence, but families from a culture that places greater value on *inter*dependence (e.g., who want their child to have very close, enduring connections with the family) may resist letting the child make choices or access materials on her own.

Scheduling

Caregivers adapt schedules and activities to meet individual children's needs within the group setting. Time schedules are flexible and smooth, dictated more by children's needs than by adults'. There is a relatively predictable sequence to the day.

○ Activities are dictated by rigid adherence to time schedules.

○ Lack of a time schedule makes the toddlers' day unpredictable.

Developmentally appropriate	In contrast

Scheduling (cont.)

Recognizing toddlers' need to repeat tasks until they master the steps and skills involved, caregivers allow each child to go at his or her own pace. Adults have time to assist a child with special needs because the rest of the children know what is expected and are engaged.

○ Caregivers lose patience with toddlers' desire for repetition.

○ Toddlers must either do things in groups according to the caregiver's plan or follow adult demands that they spend a certain amount of time on an activity.

○ Caregivers have little time for a child with special needs.

Caregivers plan walks around the neighborhood or to a park and special trips so that toddlers see many outdoor environments and experience natural settings.

○ Toddlers rarely go outside because it takes so much time for adults to get organized. Or caregivers consider toddlers too young to appreciate "field trips."

Comments on scheduling:

—Toddlers are cognitively ready to learn sequences of events, and they feel more secure when they know what will happen next in their day.

—When caregivers let children set the direction and pace of an activity, toddlers can learn on their own and practice what they are learning. It is important for adults to resist hurrying toddlers when they are engaged; their engagement frees adults up to give time to every child, including any with special needs.

—Being outside every day is important for toddlers' physical, mental, and emotional health. Fresh air is important, as is exercise, for the children's growing and developing body and brain.

Routines

The diapering/toileting, sleeping, and eating areas are separate, both for sanitation and to ensure quiet, restful areas.

○ Areas are combined and thus very noisy, distracting, and unhealthy.

Caregivers recognize that routine tasks of living, such as eating, toileting, and dressing, are important opportunities to help children learn about their world, acquire skills, and regulate their own behavior.

○ Caregivers perform for toddlers routine tasks that the children could do for themselves.

Comments on routines:

—Positive responses to children's attempts to do for themselves encourage them to continue trying. When consistently given opportunities to practice, children learn to use utensils, toilet independently, and dress themselves. Not all cultures value independence, so such families may initially think their toddlers are being neglected when caregivers don't spoon feed or dress them.

—Communication with parents about daily routines and needs should be ongoing. For example, if caregivers learn that a child didn't get enough breakfast or refused to eat anything, they can offer the child an early snack.

—During routines, caregivers need to understand and follow good practice for health, safety, nutrition, and so on.

—For more specific information, please reference the NAEYC Health and Safety accreditation criteria: "Physical Environment" and "Health."

Developmentally Appropriate Examples to Consider

Developmentally appropriate	In contrast

Routines (cont.)

Eating

Toddlers are provided snacks more frequently and in smaller portions than are older children (e.g., two morning snacks rather than preschoolers' usual single snack). Liquids are provided frequently. Children's and families' food preferences are respected.

○ Hungry children are allowed to become fussy and cranky, waiting for food that is served on a rigid schedule.

○ Caregivers use food for rewards or withhold it as punishment.

Caregivers supply utensils that toddlers can use easily for meals and snacks, such as bowls, spoons, and graduated versions of bottles and cups.

○ Children feel incompetent or frustrated because the eating utensils are too difficult for them to manage.

○ Children are expected to do things for themselves but are reprimanded for spills or accidents.

Toddlers eat in small groups at low tables. Their caregiver sits nearby to provide assistance as needed.

○ Toddlers are fed in large groups in sequence or left to manage on their own.

Napping

Toddlers can nap in the play area as long as their cots are well separated from each other and the space is cleared of play objects (e.g., stored on shelves). Caregivers plan where each toddler's cot will go according to the child's ease or difficulty in resting, distractibility, need for quiet, or length of normal nap.

○ Caregivers place cots too close together. No thought is given to planning for each toddler's sleeping needs.

Each toddler has his or her own labeled cot and bedding. Retrieving their own blankets or special stuffed toys is a part of children's nap routine.

○ Cots and sheets are used interchangeably by all children.

○ Bringing special items from home is discouraged because children "only lose them" or "just fight over them."

Caregivers establish a transition into naptime with a predictable sequence of events and a change in the environment. It begins with a quiet activity, such as reading a story. Once the cots are in place, toddlers get their stuffed toys or blankets and go to their cots. Lights are turned down, and soft music or a story tape plays for toddlers who are awake.

○ There is no transition to naptime; once toddlers are lying down, caregivers just turn off the lights, expecting children to be quiet immediately.

○ Naptime is chaotic. Some toddlers sleep; others are disruptive, wandering about the room.

Developmentally appropriate	In contrast

Routines (cont.)

Napping (cont.)

Comments on napping:

—Naptime can be difficult no matter how prepared the caregiver is. Some children may be overtired and some not tired enough. Toddlers who are feeling insecure may have a hard time relaxing enough to go to sleep.

—Some toddlers have trouble ignoring the other children. Caregivers' understanding of individual differences is key: To relax, some toddlers need visual privacy (they can't see the others), some need auditory privacy (can't hear them), and some toddlers need both, which is not easy to arrange, but creative caregivers find ways.

—In some families, toddlers never sleep alone, so they may find naptime in the program difficult. For toddlers who normally sleep in cribs, the freedom of a cot can invite them to get up and move about.

Diapering and Toileting

Caregivers work cooperatively with families in encouraging children to learn to use the toilet. When toddlers reach an age when they feel confident and unafraid to sit on a toilet seat, caregivers take them to use the toilet regularly in response to each child's biological needs, help them as needed, provide manageable clothing, and positively reinforce them.

○ Caregivers do not discuss toilet learning with families, but they impose it on children for the adults' convenience, whether children are ready or not.

○ Caregivers make children sit on the toilet for undue lengths of time.

○ Children are punished or shamed for toileting accidents.

Toddlers who are not ready to use the toilet or who have had an accident are usually diapered by the child's primary caregiver or another familiar adult. Treated as personal, one-on-one interaction, diapering builds the caregiver–toddler relationship and a sense of teamwork.

○ All toddlers are diapered by the same person, not necessarily the child's primary caregiver or a familiar adult.

○ Diapering is performed brusquely.

Comments on diapering and toileting:

—The developmental perspective on toileting focuses on individual readiness and takes a positive approach. Caregivers let the child and family take the lead on toileting, rather than following a rigid set of guidelines. Positive toileting grows naturally out of a caregiver's (and the parents') relationship with the child during diapering—if the adults treated the child as part of the team during diapering as an infant, as a toddler, the child will continue to see his or her role as cooperating with them in learning to use the toilet.

—Toddler-size toilets, which don't require children to use a stepstool, are ideal. The toilet should be in a well-lit, inviting, relatively private space. Families from cultures that start toilet training in infancy may be surprised by programs that take a more flexible and gradual approach; caregivers working with such families may be surprised that year-old babies and very young toddlers are already out of diapers.

Developmentally appropriate	In contrast

Routines (cont.)

Dressing

Toddlers' attempts to dress themselves and put on shoes are supported and positively encouraged.

○ Caregivers discourage toddlers from putting on or taking off items of clothing by themselves because "they take so long."

○ Because caregivers fail to encourage toddler-friendly clothes (e.g., no tiny buttons or laces), children struggle in learning how to dress themselves, and adults spend a lot of time helping them.

> Comments on dressing:
> —Toddlers can more feasibly learn to dress themselves when their clothes do not require a lot of fine motor precision (e.g., shoes with Velcro, pants with an elastic waist).

Reciprocal Relationships With Families

Caregivers work in partnership with parents, communicating daily to build mutual understanding and trust and to ensure each toddler's well-being and optimal development.

○ Caregivers do not seek to communicate with parents.

Caregivers respect parents as being their child's most important relationship and as having ultimate responsibility for the child's well-being and care. They focus on parents' expertise and attachment to their toddlers.

○ Caregivers set themselves up as "the experts" and cause parents to feel inadequate and peripheral to the care of their child.

Caregivers listen carefully to what parents say about their child; seek to understand parents' goals, priorities, and preferences; and show respect for cultural and family differences. They solicit and incorporate parents' knowledge in making decisions about how best to support the toddler's development or to handle problems or differences of opinion as they arise.

○ Caregivers ignore parents' concerns, or they capitulate to parent demands or preferences, even when these are at odds with developmentally appropriate practice.

○ Caregivers blame parents when children have difficulty. Or they demand that parents punish children at home for something that happened in the program.

Caregivers help parents feel good about their toddlers and their parenting (e.g., by sharing some of the positive and interesting things that happened that day).

○ Caregivers mention only problems to parents.

Developmentally appropriate	In contrast

Reciprocal Relationships With Families (cont.)

Caregivers always make parents feel welcome in the toddler program setting.

○ Caregivers communicate a competitive or patronizing attitude to parents.

○ Caregivers make parents feel in the way.

Comments on reciprocal relationships with families:

—When parents (and other family members) and caregivers take a team approach, they are able to figure out together how to solve problems and support children. Caregivers who see themselves as partners with families go out of their way to build relationships, even though there may be time constraints that make this difficult. In a team approach, caregivers spend less time trying to convince parents of anything and more time trying to understand their point of view as well as share developmentally appropriate practices with them.

—Helping parents feel good about their child's positive qualities leads to family support for those qualities. Most parents want to feel good about their child, but in some cultures, they may not want to hear that their child feels pride in herself. Such a family may instead choose to downplay a child's positive qualities and promote humility.

Policies

Health and Safety

Caregivers follow health and safety procedures, including proper hand washing methods and universal precautions to limit the spread of infectious diseases. There are clearly written sanitation procedures specific to each task or routine to help staff remember to follow procedures completely and consistently.

○ Policies and procedures to ensure a sanitary facility have not been clearly thought through and are not written down. Consequently, adults forget hand washing or other essential steps in toileting and handling food and eating utensils.

○ Caregivers are not consistent in maintaining sanitary conditions and procedures.

The space has been constructed and set up with health and safety in mind (e.g., walls are painted with lead-free, easy-to-clean paint; carpeting and other floor coverings are easy to clean; a first aid kit is kept stocked and easily accessible).

○ The space is not organized to foster toddlers' health and safety.

○ The space is clean and safe but has a sterile, institutional feel.

Comments on health and safety:

—Caregivers need training, support, and reminders to understand and consistently follow proper health and safety procedures (e.g., not letting toddlers share cups or spoons).

—For more specific information, please reference the NAEYC Health and Safety accreditation criteria: "Physical Environment" and "Health."

—See also *Healthy Young Children: A Manual for Programs* (Aronson 2012); *Model Child Care Health Policies* (Aronson 2002); and the American Academy of Pediatrics website at www.aap.org.

Developmentally appropriate	In contrast

Policies (cont.)

Staffing

Program makes every effort to hire caregivers who have training in child development/early education specific to the toddler age group. Caregivers are open to ongoing training and support in order to increase and improve their knowledge and skills. They know how to work with toddlers in groups and individually. Staff are competent in first aid.

○ Program hires caregivers who have no training in child development/early education. Or their training and experience are limited to working with older children.

○ Caregivers view toddlers as immature preschoolers rather than appreciating their unique stage of development.

○ Caregivers are unaware of what signals to look for that might indicate developmental delays or a need for evaluation.

Program hires caregivers who enjoy working with toddlers, respond warmly to their communications and needs, and demonstrate considerable patience in supporting children as they become increasingly competent and independent.

○ Program hires caregivers who view work with toddlers as a custodial chore.

○ Caregivers expect little of toddlers. Or they push children to achieve and are impatient with their struggles.

○ Caregivers take toddlers' limit testing ("No!") personally and continually get into power struggles over trivial matters.

Program limits group size and the adult:child ratio to minimize the number of adults that toddlers must relate to each day.

○ Both group size and staff:child ratio are too large to permit individual attention and constant supervision. Staffing patterns require toddlers to relate to multiple different adults during the caregiving day.

Program ensures continuity over time for each toddler's relationship with one or two primary caregivers. Child and caregiver are able to form and maintain their relationship, and each child's ongoing relationship with the other children in the group is supported.

○ Staffing patterns shift caregivers around often, from toddler to toddler or group to group.

○ Child groupings change constantly (e.g., children "graduate" to the next room and staff).

○ Each adult cares for so many children or is responsible for only one or two aspects of care (e.g., dressing), so caregivers don't spend enough time with each toddler.

○ High staff turnover results in low continuity of care and frequent disruption of toddlers' budding, satisfying attachments to caregivers.

Developmentally appropriate	In contrast

Policies (cont.)

Staffing (cont.)

Comments on staffing:

—Staff training and support are very important. Toddlerhood is a developmental stage different from either infancy or preschool age.

—Toddlers require relationship-based care and education; group size and adult:child ratio should be limited to allow for the intimate, interpersonal atmosphere and high level of supervision that toddlers require. With a small number of consistent adults to relate to, toddlers can feel safe and secure, which contributes to their learning and development. Conversely, toddlers tend to avoid attachment if caregivers come and go.

—For more specific information, please reference the NAEYC Health and Safety accreditation criteria: "Teaching" and "Teachers."

FAQs About Developmentally Appropriate Practice

Teachers administrators, parents, and policy makers ask all sorts of questions about developmentally appropriate practice. Here we briefly address the most common ones. We recognize that responses to such questions are not static. They evolve with changes in the contexts of early childhood programs and schools, the knowledge base, and the thinking of the many individuals who work in the field. So, NAEYC offers these responses not to give the final word on these questions, but rather to foster further conversations among all early childhood educators.

Do proponents of DAP think that there is only one right way to work with infants and toddlers?

Actually, developmentally appropriate practice means just the opposite. Individual children vary greatly in their development, prior experience, abilities, preferences, and interests, and there is no formula that works for them all. Moreover, to teach any child effectively, teachers must use a variety of approaches and strategies and make intentional choices about what to use in a particular situation. Good infant and toddler teachers acknowledge, support, encourage, and create challenges that extend children's learning and development. Children often pick up and imitate the behavior of those around them, and teachers are always modeling behavior, whether consciously or not. That's very indirect teaching, but it's powerful. Of course, teachers of infants and toddlers will also teach directly by giving specific information, but children should first be encouraged to see if they can figure things out themselves.

Q Is "Developmentally Appropriate Practice" a curriculum?

No, DAP is not a curriculum. It is a set of guidelines that can be used to help educators make decisions about curriculum as well as teaching strategies for supporting and promoting development and learning. *Curriculum* can be defined in many ways, but the most basic definition is usually that curriculum is the *what*—that is, the content and the plans for experiences that support development and learning. Planning curriculum that is appropriate for children is certainly one aspect of DAP, but there is not a particular curriculum that is designated as "developmentally appropriate practice."

There are a variety of early childhood curriculum approaches that are based on the underlying principles of child development and learning that undergird the NAEYC guidelines for developmentally appropriate practice. There are also many commercially developed curriculum products that reflect diverse theoretical perspectives on learning and development and provide more or less structure and support for the teacher. Principles of developmentally appropriate practice should always be applied in developing, selecting, and implementing a curriculum.

At the same time, whatever the curriculum model, it can only be truly effective and developmentally appropriate if teachers understand how children generally learn and develop, and if they adapt their teaching materials, experiences, and strategies to meet those children's individual needs. Curriculum matters, but it does not take the place of a good teacher.

Q Are developmentally appropriate programs unstructured?

The idea that there is very little or no structure in a DAP classroom is a misconception. Again, in reality the opposite is true. To be developmentally appropriate, a program must be thoughtfully structured to build on and advance children's competence. For this reason, a developmentally appropriate program is well organized in its routines and physical environment and uses a planned curriculum to guide teachers as they support children in their learning and development. The structure of a developmentally appropriate program is not rigid, however. Instead it permits adaptation for individual variation and is flexible, so as to accommodate children's interests and progress.

In the developmentally appropriate program, there is a predictable but not rigid schedule to the day, with clear limits so children learn what is acceptable behavior and what is not. Children are in an environment where they have opportunities to move freely, and within the course of the day are presented with appropriate objects, equipment, and experiences. Exercise occurs outdoors and in, and the environment is set up to foster children's climbing, balancing, and other physical skills. For infants and toddlers, physical skills are closely tied to intellectual development, and also contribute to social-emotional goals. The teacher is intentional in using the environment and everything in it to enable children to acquire important knowledge and skills.

Someone told me that in DAP classrooms, all children do is play. Is that true?

Research shows that self-initiated, teacher-supported play benefits children in many ways. When infants and toddlers play, they engage in many important tasks, such as developing and practicing newly acquired skills and regulating emotions and behaviors. As they grow out of infancy, play includes making friends, using language creatively, eventually taking turns, and learning to respond appropriately to the demands of the situation. This is why infants and toddlers need to play for a large part of the day, when they aren't otherwise involved in essential activities such as eating and diaper changing.

Play is an important part of a developmentally appropriate program. At first, young infants' play is exploratory and manipulative as they grasp, hold, mouth, and drop various play objects. Infants in groups might also explore each other while an ever watchful caregiver teaches them to be gentle. For toddlers, effective teachers often take action to enhance and support children's play and the learning that goes on in the play context. They may engage in one-on-one conversations with children and encourage pretend play with themes, roles, guidance, and props—all of which research shows is related to both language and literacy development.

But play is not the only thing that children do in developmentally appropriate programs. They also participate in enriching routines, which become important learning experiences as they engage with teachers and peers, acquire self-help skills, and learn how to help others. Toddlers may also work in small groups, listen to stories, and perhaps occasionally meet in a larger group. An important part of learning and development involves problem solving, which may happen during play or other times. Allowing infants and toddlers to solve their own problems rather than rescuing them may not fit all parents' ideas of good practice, but it is an important way for children to learn.

The flip side of the play question also arises: In light of current demands for improving learning outcomes and narrowing the achievement gap, is play still a major component of DAP?

Yes, it certainly is. The 2009 position statement says more about play than any previous statement has done (NAEYC 2009). In fact, as the relevant knowledge base has grown, there is more to say about play—its enormous value, its endangered status in today's media-intensive world, and what teachers can do to enable all children to reach the higher levels of play that are most conducive for promoting self-regulation and other aspects of development and learning.

I like to teach in my own style. Would DAP stifle my individuality as a teacher?

Teachers are individuals, just as children are. We each have our own interests, abilities, preferences, social and cultural contexts, and unique experiences that make us who we are. Developmentally appropriate practice calls for the teacher to create a caring community of learners, an important member of which is the teacher. Teachers should bring their unique selves, including their talents and interests, into the program. If a teacher is artistic, musical, literary, athletic, or whatever, she should be able to draw on her own style in her teaching, because it probably reflects her strengths.

The important thing to remember is not every child will share the teacher's preferred style. To be effective, you must understand how the *children* learn and develop, and use a variety of strategies to meet those children's individual needs as well as the needs of the group.

I think DAP makes sense, but the families I serve have different ideas about how their children should be cared for and taught. What should I do?

Begin by dropping the jargon when you communicate with families. Don't use the terms "DAP" or even "developmentally appropriate practice." Instead, have a conversation with families about your ideas, plans, and goals for the program, as well as what they want and expect.

Negotiating differences begins with you clearly understanding your own preferences and where they come from. This might take your doing some serious thinking and reflecting first. Then communicate about your point of view and listen, truly *listen,* to the family's concerns. When you and the family articulate your respective goals, it is likely that you can find common ground. Be open to learning from family members and willing to expand your view of effective, developmentally appropriate practice based on what you learn. In a successful negotiation, families also learn and change. If you just give in to parents' demands, you will lose self-respect and probably effectiveness; if parents just give in to your position, they lose their power in their relationship with you and in their children's lives. In either case, children ultimately lose. The goal is a win-win outcome in which teacher and family learn from each other and come up with a solution that works for both.

I want my child to be ready to succeed in school. Doesn't he need more than DAP in his program?

Developmentally appropriate programs richly contribute to children's learning and development. One of the well-documented research findings about high-quality, developmentally appropriate early childhood programs is that they do prepare children for later success in school, especially children living in poverty (Bowman, Donovan, & Burns 2000; Schweinhart & Weikart 1997; USDHHS 2006). A good program helps children acquire the kind of foundation they need for later school learning, gaining competencies in three key areas: mind, feelings, and body. This means that they gain thinking skills (e.g., using language effectively), learn to recognize and experience their emotions (e.g., positively using the energy that accompanies strong feelings), and learn to use their bodies effectively (e.g., gaining strength and balance). They also learn to get along with others and care about them.

In the earliest years, it's important to recognize the interconnectedness of the foundational learning areas important to later school learning—they always go together! So, if children are not making learning and developmental progress toward the important outcomes of those foundational areas, then the program is not developmentally appropriate.

I teach children with disabilities. Is there a conflict between DAP and the methods used in special education?

Children with disabilities are children first. They share most of the same developmental and learning needs and have many of the same strengths as their peers without disabilities. The DAP principles of meeting children where they are and creating challenging and achievable goals are just as important for children with disabilities. Further, we know from decades of research in early childhood special education that children with disabilities benefit most from being served in inclusive settings—that is, places where they would be found if they did not have a disability (Odom 2002; Sandall et al. 2005).

Teachers of infants and toddlers with identified disabilities should be part of a team that includes specialists and families and that develops and implements an Individualized Family Service Plan (IFSP) for the child. The plan, along with participation in the inclusive setting, should ensure that the child makes desired progress toward the shared goals of the family and the program.

My program serves children from a variety of cultures, and I'm wondering whether DAP is the best thing for them. Is DAP for all children or just for some children?

The principles of developmentally appropriate practice call for teachers to pay attention to the social and cultural contexts in which the children live and take these into account in shaping the environment for development and learning. Whatever children's prior experiences or cultural expectations are, teachers help them to make sense of new experiences. At times, this situation may require explicit teaching of limits or skills that the child has not previously encountered. Or it will require the teacher to recognize that children can acquire the same skills and ideas through different experiences and routines. For example, in some cultures, babies are spoon-fed longer than others; teachers can recognize that feeding a baby the same way her mother does will someday lead to self-feeding, though the timing may be different from what's expected by the other families in the program. Most important, the classroom must be a welcoming environment that demonstrates respect and support for all families and their children's family and cultural contexts.

I am sometimes daunted by the circumstances of children growing up in poverty. Will DAP enable them to catch up and be ready for school?

This is a good question, and the answer is "yes, but . . ." Closing the performance gap between children from families with low incomes and those from the middle class is a formidable task, and it needs to be tackled early in children's lives. Early interventions, which can even start prenatally, are crucial in closing this gap in language development and other areas (Tough 2009; USDHHS 2006). Clearly, programs serving children from families with low incomes need to give special attention to language development if children are to perform at the same level as their middle-class peers.

Without intervention, differences in children's early environments can be staggering. For example, a child in a professional family on average hears 11 million words a year, while a child in a family of low income hears just 3 million

(Hart & Risley 1995). In the earliest years, adult responses to infants' vocalizations are crucial in building early oral language skills. Babbling is the precursor to language, and adults can increase babbling by responding to it. This is important to recognize because adults who worry about vocabulary deficits tend to talk nonstop with infants, flooding them with language. However, a study of infants and mothers found that "how often a mother initiated a conversation with her child was not predictive of the language outcomes—what mattered was, if the infant initiated, whether the mom responded" (Bronson & Merryman 2009, 208). By toddlerhood, the children of high-responding mothers were six months ahead in language development compared with those of mothers who weren't so responsive. This is important information for parents and teachers. As Magda Gerber stressed, being responsive to what the infant initiates is very important, and the research backs that up.

Teachers working with dual language learners have the additional challenge of ensuring that those children continue to maintain and develop their home language. Many adults worry that learning two languages will confuse and delay language development in infants and toddlers. However, research indicates this is not true—in fact, it is very important to give special attention to supporting home language learning in infant-toddler programs (Stechuk, Burns, & Yandian. 2006). Further, as Tabors states, "What research has shown is that the bilingual children who do best in school are those who have had a strong grounding in their home language" (2008, 131).

The principles and guidelines of developmentally appropriate practice certainly should underlie all our efforts to serve all these children and their families well. If we truly meet the learners where they are and help them to reach challenging and achievable goals, as DAP requires, we will promote their learning and development to their great long-term benefit. But, as dramatically shown by evidence such as that of Hart and Risley, some children have ground to make up. So teachers need to be knowledgeable about the learning needs of the children they teach and the teaching strategies with proven success in helping such children reach higher levels of achievement.

A key fact that should also be noted is that children and families living with the many stresses of poverty typically need access to comprehensive services including health, nutrition, mental health, and social services. Early Head Start provides these, and there are other programs funded in various ways that also provide comprehensive services to families expecting a baby or who have infants and toddlers. There are not enough of them, but such programs do make a difference. Thus, advocating for these services is important for all those concerned about children's well-being.

Q **I've heard DAP is about not hurrying children, about giving them the gift of time. Is that right?**

The expression "gift of time" comes from a valid concern of not expecting too much of children too soon. Giving a child time can be both a benefit and a disservice. Let us explain.

How can time be a benefit? Infants and toddlers each have their own individual developmental timetable. If you push them to reach milestones before they are ready, they may well skip over preliminary skills—the foundations needed for that milestone. For example, you can't really teach a baby to walk. If you try, the results are an unstable walker who needs your help longer than he would otherwise. When the child can get up on his own two feet and balance by himself, he has learned just what his body can do, and progresses from there.

However, allowing for extra time can also do a child a real disservice. Why? It isn't just time that promotes development, it is also what happens while the time passes—the experiences a child has with objects and people. A baby who grows up in a deprived situation, with little opportunity to form positive attachments and explore and learn about the environment and herself, needs more than just time. And infants and toddlers who experience violence—either directly or as witnesses—especially need intervention. A DAP program geared to understanding the individual needs of infants and toddlers can make the kind of difference that just giving a child time can't do.

So DAP does not mean simply waiting until children are "ready." It means setting developmentally appropriate expectations and understanding that, although there are some biological limitations, children's learning experiences will drive their development. For example, 2-year-olds lack the fine motor skills needed to manipulate a pencil and form letters, but digging, playing with clay, and other fine motor activities build up the necessary muscles, while opportunities to scribble and draw help them get ready to write. Maturation is needed, but so is experience.

Young Children Articles

Keys to Quality Infant Care:
Nurturing Every Baby's Life Journey

Alice Sterling Honig

Teachers of infants need a large bunch of key ideas and activities of all kinds to unlock in each child the treasures of loving kindness, thoughtful and eloquent use of language, intense active curiosity to learn, willingness to cooperate, and the deep desire to work hard to master new tasks. Here are some ideas that teachers can use during interactions with infants to optimize each child's development.

Get to Know Each Baby's Unique Personality

At 4 months, Luci holds her hands in front of her face and turns them back and forth so she can see the curious visual difference between the palms and backs. Jackson, an 8-month-old, bounces happily in accurate rhythm as his teacher bangs on a drum and chants, "Mary had a little lamb whose fleece was white as snow!" Outdoors, 1-year-old Jamie sits in an infant swing peering down at his feet sticking out of the leg holes. How interesting! Those are the same feet he has watched waving in the air while being diapered and has triumphantly brought to his mouth to chew on.

Teachers can tune in to each child's special personality—especially the child's temperament. There are three primary, mostly inborn, styles of

This article was first published in the September 2010 issue of *Young Children.*

Alice Sterling Honig, PhD, professor emerita of child development, licensed psychologist, and author of nearly 600 articles and more than a dozen books, conducts QIC (a quality infant/toddler caregiving workshop) each summer at Syracuse University.

temperament (Honig 1997). Some babies are more low-key; they tend to be slow to warm up to new caregivers, new foods, and new surroundings. They need reassuring hand-holding and more physical supports to try a new activity. Others are more feisty and sometimes irritable. They tend to be impetuous, intense in their emotional reactions, whether of anger or of joy. Easygoing babies are typically friendly, happy, accept new foods and caregivers without much fuss, and adapt fairly quickly and more flexibly after experiencing distress or sudden change. Try to find out whether each baby in your care tends to be low-key and slow to warm up *or* mostly feisty and intense *or* easygoing. A caring adult's perceptive responses in tune with individual temperament will ease a child's ability to adapt and flourish in the group setting.

Physical Loving

Your body is a safe haven for an infant. Indeed, some babies will stay happy as a clam when draped over a shoulder, across your belly as you rock in a rocking chair, or especially for a very young baby, snuggled in a sling or carrier for hours. As Montagu (1971) taught decades ago, babies need *body loving:* "To be tender, loving, and caring, human beings must be tenderly loved and cared for in their earliest years. . . . caressed, cuddled, and comforted" (138).

As you carry them, some babies might pinch your neck, lick your salty arm, pull at your hair, tug at eyeglasses, or show you in other ways how pow-

erfully important your body is as a sacred and special playground. Teach gentleness by calmly telling a baby you need your glasses on to read a story. Use the word *gently* over and over and over. Dance cheek-to-cheek with a young child in your arms to slow waltz music—good for dreary days! Also carry the baby while you do a routine task such as walking to another room to get something.

Provide lap and touch times generously to nourish a child's sense of well-being. Slowly caress a baby's hair. Rub a tense shoulder soothingly. Kiss one finger and watch as a baby offers every other finger to kiss. Rock a child with your arms wrapped around him for secure comfort. Babies learn to become independent as we confirm and meet their dependency needs in infancy. A sense of

well-being and somatic certainty flows from cherishing adults who generously hold, caress, and drape babies on shoulders and tummies.

Create Intimate Emotional Connections

Scan the environment so you can be close to every baby. Notice the quiet baby sitting alone, mouthing a toy piece and rocking back and forth with vacant eyes. Notice shy bids for attention, such as a brief smile with lowered lids. The child with an easy or cautious temperament needs your loving attention as much as the one who impulsively climbs all over you for attention.

Shine admiring eyes at the children, whether a baby is cooing as she lies in her crib, creeping purposefully toward a toy she desires, or feeding herself happily with messy fingers. Speak each child's name lovingly and frequently. Even if they are fussing, most babies will quiet when you chant and croon their names.

Although babies do not understand the meanings of the words, they do understand *tonal* nuances and love when your voice sounds admiring, enchanted with them, and happy to be talking with them. While diapering, tell the baby he is so delicious and you love his plump tummy and the few wispy hairs on that little head. Watch him thrust out his legs in delight on the diapering table. Your tone of voice entrances him into a deep sense of pleasure with his own body (Honig 2002).

Harmonizing Tempos

Tempo is important in human activities and is reflected in how abruptly or smoothly adults carry out daily routines. Because adults have so many tasks to do, sometimes we use impatient, too-quick motions—for example, while dressing a baby to play outdoors. When dressing or feeding, more leisurely actions are calming. They signal to children that we have time for them. Rub backs slowly and croon babies into soothing sleep.

A baby busily crawling across the rug sees a toy, grasps it, then plops himself into a sitting position to examine and try to pull it apart. He slowly looks back and forth at the toy as he leisurely passes it from hand to hand. He has no awareness that a teacher is about to interrupt because she is in a hurry to get him dressed because his daddy is coming to pick him up. Young children need time and cheerful supports to finish up an activity in which they are absorbed. If they are hurried, they may get frustrated and even have a tantrum.

Enhance Courage and Cooperation

Your presence can reassure a worried baby. Stay near and talk gently to help a child overcome his fear of the small infant slide. Pascal sits at the top, looking uncertain. Then he checks your face for a go-ahead signal, for reassurance that he can bravely try to slide down this slide that looks so long to him. Kneeling at the bottom of the slide, smile and tell him that you will be there to catch him when he is ready to slide down.

Be available as a "refueling station"—Margaret Mahler's felicitous term (Kaplan 1978). Sometimes a baby's independent learning adventure comes crashing down—literally. Your body and your lap provide the emotional support from which a baby regains courage to tackle the learning adventure again.

Create loving rituals during daily routines of dressing, bath times, nap times, feeding times. Babies like to know what will happen and when and where and how. Babies have been known to refuse lunch when their familiar, comfortable routines were changed. At cleanup times, older babies can be more flexible and helpful if you change some chores into games. Through the use of singsong chants, putting toys away becomes an adventure in finding the big fat blocks that need to be placed together on a shelf and then the skinny blocks that go together in a different place.

Address Stress

Young children need time and cheerful supports to finish up an activity in which they are absorbed. If they are hurried, they may get frustrated and even have a tantrum.

Attachment research shows that babies who develop secure emotional relationships with a teacher have had their distress signals noticed, interpreted correctly, and responded to promptly and appropriately (Honig 2002). At morning arrival times, watch for separation anxiety. Sometimes holding and wordlessly commiserating with a baby's sad feelings can help more than a frenzied attempt to distract her (Klein, Kraft, & Shohet 2010). As you become more expert at interpreting a baby's body signals of distress and discomfort, you will become more sensitively attuned in your responses (Honig 2010).

Learn developmental milestones. Learning developmental norms helps teachers figure out when to wonder, when to worry, and when to relish and feel overjoyed about a child's milestone accomplishments. Day and night toilet learning can be completed anywhere from 18 months to 5 years. This is a *wide* time window for development. In contrast, learning to pick up a piece of cereal from a high chair tray with just thumb and forefinger in a fine pincer grasp is usually completed during a *narrow* time window well before 13 months. By 11 months, most babies become expert at using just the first two fingers.

Hone your detective skills. If a baby is screaming and jerking knees up to his belly, you might suspect a painful gas bubble. Pick up the baby and jiggle and thump his back until you get that burp up. What a relief, for you as well as baby. Maybe an irritable, yowling baby just needs to be tucked in quietly and smoothly for a nap after an expert diaper change. Suppose baby is crying and thrashing about, and yet he has been burped and diapered. Use all your detective skills to determine the cause. Is it a hot day? He might be thirsty. A drink of water can help him calm down.

Notice stress signs. Scan a child's body for stress signs. Dull eyes can signal the need for more intimate loving interactions. Tense shoulders and a grave look often mean that a child is afraid or worried (Honig 2010). Compulsive rocking can mean a baby feels forlorn. Watch for lonesomeness and wilting.

Some babies melt down toward day's end. They need to be held and snuggled. Murmur sweet reassurances and provide a small snack of strained applesauce to soothe baby's taste buds and worries. Check his body from top to bottom for signs of stresses or tensions, such as eyes avoiding contact, teeth grinding, fingernail chewing, frequently clenched fists, so that you can develop an effective plan for soothing. Be alert, and tend to children's worrisome bodily signs; these will tell you what you need to know long before children have enough language to share what was stressful (Honig 2009).

Play Learning Games

Parents and teachers are a baby's preferred playmates. While playing learning games with infants, pay attention to their actions. Ask yourself if the game has become so familiar and easy that it is time to "dance up the developmental ladder" (Honig 1982) and increase the game's challenge. Or perhaps the game is still too baffling and you need to "dance down" and simplify the activity so that the child can succeed.

Provide safe mirrors at floor level and behind the diapering table so children can watch and learn about their own bodies. Hold babies in your arms up to a mirror so they can to reach out and pat the face in the mirror. Lying on the floor in front of a securely attached safety mirror, a young child twists and squirms to get an idea of where his body begins and ends.

Your body can serve as a comforting support for some early learning activities. Sit an infant on your lap and watch as he coordinates vision and grasp to reach and hold a toy you are dangling. Babies love "Peekaboo! I see you!" These games nurture the development of object permanence—the understanding that objects still exist even when they are out of sight. Peekaboo games also symbolically teach that even when a special adult is not seen, that dear person will reappear.

Provide physical play experiences. Play pat-a-cake with babies starting even before 6 months. As you gently hold a baby's hands and bring them out and then back together, chant slowly and joyously, "Pat-a-cake, pat-a-cake, baker's man; bake me a cake just as fast as you can. Pat it, and roll it, and mark it with a *B,* and put it in the oven for [baby's name] and me." Smile with joy as you guide the baby's hands rhythmically and slowly through the game, and use a high-pitched voice as you emphasize her name in the singsong chant. Over the next months, as soon as you begin chanting the words, the baby will begin to bring hands to the midline and do the hand motions that belong with this game. Babies who are 9 to 11 months old will even start copying the hand-rolling motions that belong with this game.

To encourage learning, try to arrange games with more physical actions. Sit on the floor with your toes touching the baby's toes, then model how to roll a ball back and forth.

Introduce sensory experiences. Safe sensory and tactile experiences are ideal for this age group. As he shifts a toy from hand to hand, turns it over, pokes, tastes, bangs, and even chews on it, a baby uses his senses to learn about the toy's physical properties. Teachers can blow bubbles so babies can reach for and crawl after them. Provide playdough made with plenty of salt to discourage children from putting it in their mouths. Older babies enjoy exploring finger paints or nontoxic tempera paint and fat brushes.

Play sociable games. Give something appealing to a seated baby. Put out your hand, smile, and say "Give it to me, please." The baby might chew on

the "gift," such as a safe wooden block or chunky plastic cylinder peg. After the baby passes it to you, say thank you, then give the object back with a smile. Give-and-take games with you are a sociable pleasure for babies and teach them turn-taking skills that are crucial for friendly social interchanges years later.

Seated on a chair, play a bouncing game, with the baby's back resting snuggly against your tummy. After you stop bouncing and chanting "Giddyup, horsie," a baby often bounces on his or her tush as if to remind you to start this game over and over. An older baby vigorously demands "More horsie!" to get you to restart this game. Babies

Focus on Infants and Toddlers

enjoy kinesthetic stimulation too, such as when you swing them gently in a baby swing. A baby will grin with glee as you pull or push him in a wagon around the room or playground.

Observe Babies' Ways of Exploring and Learning

Observe a baby to learn what and how she is learning, then adapt the activity to offer greater challenge. Observation provides information that lets teachers determine when and how to arrange for the next step in a child's learning experience. Watch quietly as a baby tries with determination to put the round wood top piece for a ring stack set on the pole. His eyes widen in startled amazement as he gradually realizes that when the hole does not go through the middle, then that piece will not go down over the pole—a frustrating but important lesson. Calmly, a teacher can demonstrate how to place the piece on top of the pole while using simple words to describe how this piece is different. She can also gently guide the baby's hands so he feels successful at placing the piece on top.

Enhance Language and Literacy in Everyday Routines

Talk back and forth with babies; respond to their coos and babbles with positive talk. When the baby vocalizes, tell her, "What a terrific talker you are. Tell me some more."

The diapering table is a fine site for language games. With young babies, practice "parentese"—a high-pitched voice, drawn-out vowels, and slow and simple talk. This kind of talk fires up the brain neurons that carry messages to help a baby learn (Doidge 2007). Cascades of chemicals and electrical signals course down the baby's neural pathways. A baby responds when you are an attentive and delighted talking partner. Pause so the baby gets a turn to talk too, and bring the game to a graceful close when baby fatigue sets in.

Talk about body parts on dolls, stuffed animals, yourself, and the babies in the room. Talk about what the baby sees as you lift her onto your lap and then onto your shoulders. Talk at mealtimes. Use every daily routine as an opportunity to enhance oral language (Honig 2007).

Daily reading is an intimate one-on-one activity that young babies deeply enjoy in varied spaces and at varied times of the day (Honig 2004). Hook your babies on books as early as possible. Frequent shared picture-book experiences

> Mastery experiences arranged in thoughtful doses bring much pleasure, such an eagerness to keep on exploring, trying, and learning.

are priceless gifts. Early pleasurable reading experiences empower success in learning to read years later in grade school (Jalongo 2007).

Cuddle with one or several children as you read and share books together every day. Use dramatic tones along with loving and polite words. You are the master of the story as you read aloud. Feel free to add to or to shorten picture-book text according to a particular child's needs. Group reading times can be pleasurable when infants lean against you as you sit on the rug and share a picture book. Teachers often prefer the intimacy of individual reading times with babies (Honig & Shin 2001). Individual reading can help a tense or fussy baby relax in your lap as he becomes deeply absorbed in sharing the picture-book experience.

Encourage Mastery Experiences

Children master many linguistic, physical, and social skills in the first years of life. Watch the joy of mastery and self-appreciation as a baby succeeds at a task, such as successfully placing Montessori cylinders into their respective sockets. Babies enjoy clapping for their own efforts. Mastery experiences arranged in thoughtful doses bring much pleasure, such an eagerness to keep on exploring, trying, and learning. Watch the baby's joy as he proudly takes a long link chain out of a coffee can and then stuffs it slowly back in the can. He straightens his shoulders with such pride as he succeeds at this game of finding a way to put a long skinny chain into a round container with a small diameter opening.

Vygotsky taught that the *zone of proximal development* is crucial for adult–child coordination in learning activities. You the teacher are so important in helping a child to succeed when a task may be slightly too difficult for the child to solve alone. Hold the baby's elbow steady when she feels frustrated while trying to stack one block on top of another. For a difficult puppy puzzle, a teacher taped down a few of the pieces so a baby could succeed in getting the puppy's tail and head pieces in the right spaces. If a baby has been struggling with a slippery nesting cup for a while, just steady the stack of cups so he can successfully insert a smaller cup into the next largest one.

Promote Socioemotional Skills

Babies learn empathy and friendliness from those who nurture them. Empathy involves recognizing and feeling the distress of another and trying to help in some way. A young baby who sees another baby crying may look worried and suck his thumb to comfort himself. Fifteen-month-old Michael tussles over a toy with Paul, who starts to cry. Michael looks worried and lets go of the toy so Paul has it. As Paul keeps crying, Michael gives him his own teddy bear. But Paul continues crying. Michael pauses, then runs to the next room and gets Paul's security blanket for him. And Paul stops crying (Blum 1987).

Friendliness includes making accommodations so children can play together. For example, move a child over to make room for a peer, or make

When teachers showed deeply respectful caregiving, then they observed that babies did develop early empathy and internalize the friendly interactions they had experienced.

Focus on Infants and Toddlers

overtures to invite other babies to engage in peer play. Perhaps they could take turns toddling in and out of a cardboard house. Babies act friendly when they sit near each other and companionably play with toys, happy to be close together. McMullen and colleagues (2009) observed that positive social-emotional interactions were rare in some infant rooms. But when teachers showed deeply respectful caregiving, then they observed that babies did develop early empathy and internalize the friendly interactions they had experienced. One teacher is described below:

> Her wonderful gentle manner, the way she speaks to the babies, how they are all her friends . . . only someone who utterly respects and values babies could put that kind of effort into this the way she does, almost like she is setting a beautiful table for honored guests each and every morning. (McMullen et al. 2009, 27)

Conclusion

Later in life, a baby will not remember your specific innumerable kindly caring actions in the earliest years. However, a child's *feelings* of being lovable and cherished will remain a body-memory for life. These feelings of having been loved will permeate positive emotional and social relationships decades later.

Keep your own joy pipes open. How brief are the years of babyhood. All too soon young children grow into the mysterious world of teenagers who prefer hanging out with peers to snuggling on an adult lap. Reflect with deep personal satisfaction on your confidence and delight in caring for tiny ones—hearing the first words, seeing the joy at a new accomplishment, watching the entranced look of an upturned face as you tell a story, feeling the trust as a baby sleepily settles onto your lap for refreshment of spirit, for a breath of the loving comfort that emanates from your body.

Life has grown more complicated in our technological, economically difficult, and more and more urbanized world. But you, the teacher, remain each baby's priceless tour guide into the world of "growing up"! You gently take each little person by the hand—literally and figuratively—and lure each and every baby into feeling the wonder and the somatic certainty of being loved, lovable, and cherished so that each baby can fully participate in the adventure of growing, loving, and learning.

Your nurturing strengthens a baby's determination to keep on learning, keep on cooperating, keep on being friendly, and keep on growing into a loving person—first in the world of the nursery and later in the wider world. You can give no greater gift to a child than to be the best guide possible as each child begins his or her unique life journey.

Rituals and Routines: Supporting Infants and Toddlers and Their Families

Linda Gillespie and Sandra Petersen

Josh brings Eliana, 20 months, into the family child care provider's home. Sherita greets Josh and Eliana with a warm "Good morning!" Eliana buries her head in her father's shoulder. Sherita pats Eliana on the back and says, "It feels so good to snuggle with Daddy." Josh tells Sherita how Eliana slept and what she had for breakfast. Eliana peeks at Sherita, and Sherita says, "I see you looking at me! Come, let me hold you while Daddy leaves for work. You know what to do: give him a kiss and a hug, and then we will go to the window. Watch—when Daddy gets to the car, he's going to turn around and wave to you." Eliana watches for her daddy to turn around and wave, then waves back.

Morning arrivals didn't always go this smoothly for Eliana and her father. When Eliana first came to Sherita's program, she had a very hard time letting her father leave and he had a hard time leaving. Sherita suggested that she and Josh think about a ritual to perform every morning when he left. Eliana could feel some control over this transition (or at least an understanding of her own role), and that might make it easier for both of them to say good-bye.

Josh suggested the strategy described in the vignette because it was what he and his partner did when they left Eliana at home with a baby-sitter. In the beginning, Eliana still cried. But over time and with patience, this daily ritual smoothed the way for parting from her dad at the family child care home.

What Are Routines?

The words *routine* and *ritual* are sometimes used interchangeably. Yet there are some important differences. Routines are repeated, predictable events that provide a foundation for the daily tasks in a child's life. Teachers can create a predictable routine in early childhood settings for infants and toddlers, and they can individualize those routines to match children's needs for sleeping and eating and to support children's development of self-regulation. Individualizing a routine means that the sequence is the same but the actions and timing may vary to accommodate the needs of individual children.

A typical schedule for infants and toddlers consists of arrival, playtime, snack, lunch, naptime, snack, and departure, with diapering taking place when needed and diaper checks at scheduled times throughout the day. Within this schedule, individual children arrive at different times, nap for different periods, eat when hungry, and so on. But the schedule of events remains consistent, providing a basic framework for the day. The familiar pattern helps infants and toddlers know what to expect and when to expect it. However, even when routines are consistent and predictable, a ritual can ease or enhance aspects of routines to make them more manageable and meaningful to the child and the caregiver.

What Are Rituals?

Rituals can be defined as special actions that help us navigate emotionally important events or transitions in our lives as well as enhance aspects of our daily routines to deepen our connections and relationships. For adults, rituals are sometimes associated with events like weddings, funerals, holidays, and religious practices. They provide a way to acknowledge the importance of such events and are usually comforting.

In early childhood settings, rituals can be developed between a parent and child or a teacher and child to ease or enrich emotionally loaded moments such as separations. A ritual is a special practice that helps a child accept aspects of a routine, even an individualized routine, that are stressful. In the opening vignette, the parting ritual that takes place within the arrival routine provides a bridge for the emotionally challenging experience of saying good-bye.

The time, predictability, and reliable emotional tone of rituals give the child, parent, and caregiver a sense of comfort and control. They help the child manage, or regulate, the unsettling feelings evoked by change and draw the child and the parent or caregiver closer with each reassuring repetition. Rituals support emotional self-regulation by offering young children a way to manage their strong emotions during a stressful time.

Because rituals are attuned to a child's individual needs, age, and family culture, they are developmentally appropriate. Each ritual is an individual set of practices for a particular child and her family or teacher. Eliana's ritual matches her stage of development. It would not work with a 6-month-old, whose memory would not be developed enough to hold a sequence of events in his mind.

Rituals are culturally appropriate because families help create them by sharing information about their ways of handling specific routines or emotionally challenging events. For example, a caregiver engaged in the routine of hand washing with Bobby (10 months) sings the ABC song to him, so that Bobby washes his hands for the required 30 seconds. She uses this song because it is the song Bobby's mother uses at home. For Eric, 30 months, she sings a song about the bubbles going down the drain, a ritual they developed together to make that 30 seconds fly by. These simple rituals around hand washing help deepen her relationship with each child and make even the mundane meaningful for both child and adult.

Rituals are not just about making transitions easier for an infant; they are also about helping the special adults in the infant's life. Donald Winnicott, a pediatrician and renowned psychiatrist, stated,

> There is no such thing as a baby . . . [there is] a *baby and someone*. A baby cannot exist alone, but is essentially part of a relationship. ([1964] 1987, 88)

This article was first published in the September 2012 issue of *Young Children* in the column Rocking and Rolling: Supporting Infants, Toddlers, and Their Families.

Linda Gillespie, MS, has worked for ZERO TO THREE for the past 10 years and has been in the early childhood field for the past 35 years. Linda coordinates the writing of the Rocking and Rolling column in *Young Children*.

Sandra Petersen, MA, has worked for ZERO TO THREE for the past 13 years and has been in the early childhood field for the past 40 years, during which she has coauthored several books.

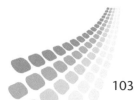

Rituals can provide support to that important someone in a child's life. Josh felt respected when Sherita enlisted his support in easing Eliana's transitions into her care, taking into consideration his experiences and practices. Rituals, when created by parent, child, and teacher together, respect each person's feelings. Therefore, they support the goal of creating and deepening the strong connections between parents and their children as well as between parents and their children's teachers. Over time, the morning parting ritual may change as Eliana adjusts to Sherita's family child care program and develops new ways to meet her need for security and control. This ritual will have provided a stepping stone toward her new understanding.

Rituals are intentional ways of approaching a routine, with careful consideration of the needs of the individual within the routine. For early childhood professionals, they are a way to connect on a deeper level with families and their children. Rituals and routines work together to create secure environments that nurture relationships between infants and their caregivers. They strengthen the bond between parents and child as well as create a partnership between parents and their child's teacher.

Think About It

• What role do you see rituals playing in your life?

• What is a ritual that has been particularly helpful to you? Why?

Try It

• Think about the children in your care. In what ways do you support their transitions throughout the day?

• Talk with families about the rituals they practice at home. Bath time and bedtime may be routine until a young child suddenly worries about the dark or about going down the drain. At that point, the adult might use a special ritual to help the child manage his fears.

Rocking and Rolling is written by infant/toddler specialists and contributed to *Young Children* by ZERO TO THREE, a nonprofit organization working to promote the health and development of infants and toddlers by translating research and knowledge into a range of practical tools and resources for use by the adults who influence the lives of young children.

Enhancing Practice With Infants and Toddlers From Diverse Language and Cultural Backgrounds

Karen N. Nemeth and Valeria Erdosi

On Meili's first day at the center, her mother carries the 18-month-old into the classroom, whispering in Mandarin to the little girl. As she sets Meili down, the mom nervously smiles and nods to the teacher, then walks out the door. Not surprisingly, little Meili starts to cry. She runs after her mother, but the door has already closed. The adults try to comfort and distract Meili, but she doesn't understand a word they say. Meili has no idea when or if her mother will ever be back.

Many infants and toddlers whose families speak languages other than English have similar experiences when entering early childhood programs. While you think about Meili's stressful experience, imagine also what her mother must feel. She will be thinking of her daughter's desperate cries all day. When she returns to pick Meili up, the mother's lack of English skills will make it impossible for her to get information about how her daughter fared that first scary day. But what if this scenario were approached in a different way?

At The King's Daughters Day School, in Plainfield, New Jersey, Meili, a newcomer to the infant/toddler room, was greeted with a few comforting words in Mandarin, even though the teachers speak mostly English. The teachers had asked Meili's parents about a few of her favorite songs so they could use them to help Meili feel more welcome and comfortable in her new surroundings. And when Meili's mother returned to pick up her daughter, a teacher showed her some digital photos of Meili happily playing during the day. A few simple steps can make all the difference in the experiences of children and families who bring different languages to infant and toddler care.

As infant/toddler programs encounter growing diversity, they need to reenvision the impact they have on children and families in all areas of practice, from recruiting new enrollees to stocking classrooms to changing the ways adults interact with children and families with different languages and from different cultures. What happens on the first day can set the stage for a family's involvement in a program.

The director and staff at The King's Daughters Day School, an NAEYC-Accredited early childhood program, take that responsibility very seriously. As one of the oldest child development programs in the United States (established in 1906), it holds a respected position in the small but diverse city of Plainfield. (Learn more about the center at www.thekingsdaughtersdayschool.org/aboutus/history.html.) The day school serves children from infancy through

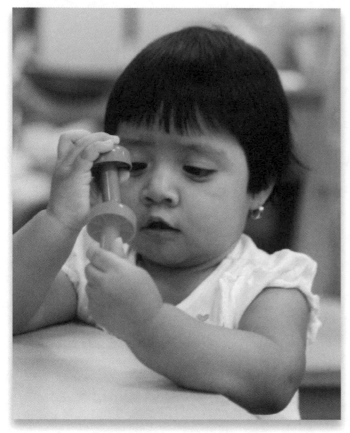

school age, and there are 55 children in its five classrooms for infants and toddlers who can walk. At this writing, 60 percent of these children come from families with first languages other than English, including Spanish, Mandarin, Urdu, and indigenous South American dialects.

When an infant is separated from his parents and left in a new place, in the care of unfamiliar adults who speak a different language, all kinds of adjustments are necessary. A new language is only part of the picture. It is important to remember that "language is a cognitive process that is influenced by all domains of development, including motor, social, and emotional. Language acquisition is also influenced by the context in which the child grows, including family, the community, and the culture in which he or she lives" (Fort & Stechuk 2008, 24). Effective, developmentally appropriate strategies for supporting infants and toddlers who are dual language learners take into account all of these factors.

The home language is a child's connection to the love, nurturing, and lessons learned in the family context. Strengthening the bond between parent and child requires continual support of the home language. There are also cognitive advantages to building the home language while the child learns English. Research demonstrates that children who grow up bilingual have advanced self-regulation skills and advanced metalinguistic skills (Yoshida 2008). Growing up with two languages helps a child better understand how language works in general because she has to be more conscious of the features and rules of each of her languages. This understanding makes children more successful as language learners.

Parents and teachers need to share a common understanding and vision for rearing children with all the advantages of the families' rich cultural and linguistic heritage while also exposing the children to English (Notari-Syverson 2006). Teachers, home visitors, family child care monitors, college professors, program directors, trainers, nannies, consultants, therapists, early intervention providers, pediatricians, and social workers need strategies to support the development of very young children with unique cultural traditions in bilingual environments (Nemeth 2012).

All infants and toddlers need experiences that nurture, support, and teach their home language and culture, because research shows that this foundation is an important contributor to children's potential success in learning English. Even for infants, full immersion in an English-only program that reduces their experiences in their home language does not offer learning or developmental advantages (August & Shanahan 2006). Defining a commitment to addressing the language needs of each child in the program must be a team effort involving everyone who works or volunteers at the center, beginning with the leader

This article was first published in the September 2012 issue of *Young Children*.

Karen Nemeth, MEd, is an author and consultant who focuses on teaching young children who are DLLs, providing resources at www. languagecastle.com. She wrote the NAEYC book *Basics of Supporting Dual Language Learners*.

Valeria Erdosi, MS, is the executive director of the King's Daughters Day School in Plainfield, New Jersey, and is a Bank Street College graduate.

Focus on Infants and Toddlers

or director. The developmentally appropriate strategies in this article address these key points.

Building Connections With New Children and Families

Every building needs a good foundation. The best way to build strong and mutually beneficial relationships with new and diverse families is to lay the foundation before those families enter the program. One way to get started is to build in time for parents to come to the program with their child for a few hours before leaving the child on a regular basis. The King's Daughters Day School asks parents to spend three mornings in the program with their child before the child officially starts. Here are some other ways to connect with diverse families.

Reach out to diverse families in the community. Letting families know that your program is prepared to welcome different languages and cultures is good for business. It also sets the stage for a positive relationship with each potential client. The King's Daughters Day School prints fliers in English and Spanish and displays them at cultural festivals, public library branches, and other public locations.

Present a welcoming first impression that celebrates diversity. To help families feel they have chosen the right program, pictures and languages on signs and displays should reflect the languages and cultures of the community. The school lines its driveway with small signs that say hello in different languages. Its entry hall displays photos of the diverse children who attend. Information for families is trimmed to as few words as possible, then translated into two or more languages, as the population requires.

Practicing With Chopsticks

At The King's Daughters Day School, teachers plan a number of activities around the use of chopsticks. This is a wonderful example of helping all children become comfortable with a utensil that is commonplace in some cultures yet unheard of in others. All children benefit from practicing fine motor skills with chopsticks, pinching them to pick up small items and later using them to eat. Toddlers can easily use chopsticks if the sticks are attached at the top with small rubber bands. Other utensils from different cultures, such as a tostonera (a plantain press, for making tostones) from Cuba, help toddlers build skills and cultural awareness at the school.

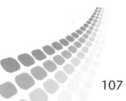

Prepare before the child starts in your program. When you get to know each new family, be sure to learn exactly what language and dialect the family speaks at home. This will help you add appropriate classroom materials so the child sees himself reflected in the books, displays, and toys. Parents will also be more at ease if they see their language and some familiar images when they drop off their child on the first day. This can be a little difficult, but it evolves over time as families and staff build relationships.

A new child's primary caregiver should learn at least a few words in the family's home language before the child starts. Some programs send home a list of 10 to 15 key words and ask parents to make an audio recording in their home language or spell the words phonetically. If this does not work out, search online for translations. *Hello, up, down, change, diaper, clean, eat, juice, bottle, gentle, yes, no, more, hurt, mommy, daddy, outside, shoes, coat,* and *buckle* might be some words for your list. Knowing these words means that the teacher can say them to the child and recognize them if the child tries to communicate in his home language.

Help the family start in your program with confidence. Provide a list of items they should send in with their child—represent the items by photos to make sure the message is clear. Take the family on a tour of the center so the parents, other family members, and the child will feel at home.

Give a special welcome on the first day. It is most important to pause and focus on welcoming a new family with uncertain English skills, no matter how hectic sign-in time is. Say hello in the family's language, and be sure to pronounce the child's name correctly. Take a moment to hold the child and look at her. Does she have a runny nose you need to ask about? Does she appear sleepy or hungry? With a little extra effort and some nonverbal communication, a teacher can make important connections with the child and the parents. The teacher can demonstrate a successful drop-off experience—not too abrupt and not too drawn out. This is much easier to achieve if a parent or other family member has spent a few mornings in the program. A happy drop-off eliminates the infant's and family member's anxiety and the loneliness of not being able to communicate.

Equip the environment for diverse infants and toddlers. Representing each child's language and culture throughout the room is consistent with developmentally appropriate practice. This is important for children's self-esteem, and exposure to images from diverse cultures is valuable for all children. Visit the public library to find board books in the languages you need. Create posters using photos of the children's recognizable surroundings, such as their homes and families, the corner grocery, or the local park. Have diverse faces and skin colors in the doll area, the puzzle rack, and the small toy shelf. Represent familiar ethnic foods and cooking tools or other artifacts in the kitchen area. Labels in key areas of the room should have the words in the languages the children use. Even better, post phonetic spellings of key words in the different locations to remind teachers how to talk about play using the children's home languages.

Linguistically and Culturally Appropriate Practices

When teachers care for children who speak different languages they must think deeply and intentionally about how they use language with infants in general. Because the home language is so important to each child's family strength, identity development, and language/literacy learning, teachers have to learn how to support both the home language and some English learning. Here are some developmentally appropriate strategies to support all of these aspects of multilingual learning.

Foster a close teacher–child relationship. With different languages in an infant/toddler group, it is especially important that each child have a primary caregiver. Helping a child to navigate the learning of two or more languages requires the teacher to have a close relationship and a deep understanding of the infant or toddler. The teacher needs to be expert at reading the child's nonverbal signals, and the child has to be close enough to the teacher to understand the teacher's nonverbal signals as well.

Schedule home language and English use around routines. Be clear about separating the use of the two languages in a predictable way. Plan how and when you will use the child's language and how and when you will use English each day. Some programs use English during play and use home languages during meals and snacks. Some programs use one language in the morning and the other in the afternoon. Even if a teacher is not fluent enough in the child's language to be able to devote half the day to its use, it is still important for him to learn key words—for example, the vocabulary needed to always use the home language at changing time and for morning greeting.

With a little extra effort and some nonverbal communication, a teacher can make important connections with the child and the parents.

Stick with one language at a time. When you say a word in two languages, a child usually focuses on one language or the other. Instead, rely on tone of voice, body language, pictures, gestures, and props to make sure the child understands the words in the language you are using.

Staff at The King's Daughters Day School often use American Sign Language (ASL) as a gestural support to enhance spoken language. Teachers learn the signs from the many websites, books, and DVDs (available commercially and in libraries) that feature baby sign language. The advantage of using ASL signs is that one teacher's gesture for *eat* or *more* or *drink* is the same as the next teacher's, so the child can understand and use the same signs no

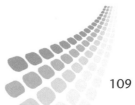

matter where she is—in the program or beyond (Goodwyn, Acredolo, & Brown 2000). As a child tries to make sense of the words you are saying about changing his diaper, signing *change* helps him see the links between the English words and the home language words connected to the same activity.

Specialize in rich home language experiences. When an adult is fluent in the home language of a child, he should plan times to use that language—and then use it with all the richness and interest that we know is critical to building early language and literacy. In some classrooms, bilingual staff use their other language only to manage the behavior of the young dual language learners, and all of the "teaching" occurs in English. Instead, staff should use their other languages in positive, engaging ways. Research shows that a strong foundation in the home language contributes to the successful acquisition of English (August & Shanahan 2006). The better you support the home language, the more you are building a foundation for effective learning of English.

Be creative and imaginative. If a primary caregiver does not speak a child's home language, she can still support it by bringing in CDs (don't be afraid to ask parents) and singing songs in the language. Try using simple recorded stories or apps for smartphones or tablets that tell stories in different languages. It is essential to interact with the infant or toddler while listening to and watching media. Hold the child in your lap and repeat the interesting words and comment on the pictures. Welcome classroom volunteers—family members or community helpers—to spend time with the children. (If you do so, first give the volunteers a little training about how you expect them to interact with the infants and toddlers. See "Provide an Orientation for Classroom Volunteers.")

Based on the research of Patricia Kuhl (2010), we know that infants as young as 6 to 8 months can benefit from just a few hours a week of language support if it is delivered in person by a nurturing and familiar visitor. Kuhl's research shows that if that weekly language interaction is replaced by video or audio recordings of the same language, infants in that 6-to-8-month age range learn none of the language. With infants and toddlers, the only effective way to use televised or recorded language is for the adult to use it with the child or for the adult to use it for herself, as a tool to learn the words she can use with the child.

Support English. A solid foundation in language and preliteracy skills is critical for the development and school readiness of every child. What is

Provide an Orientation for Classroom Volunteers

When parents or other community members who speak a second language decide to volunteer in the classroom, it is important to provide an orientation session. They may never have seen a working infant/toddler classroom before. They need guidance about the value of using their home language to talk, describe, ask questions, read, sing, and pretend with the children.

Focus on Infants and Toddlers

important is that each young child grow, learn, and play every day in an environment filled with interesting words, one-on-one nurturing interactions, expression, wonder, discovery, and patience. In the first three years, it is possible that having this environment completely in a non-English language will help the later learning of English (August & Shanahan 2006). Having this environment almost entirely in English does not make English learning quicker or better in the long run (August & Shanahan 2006). Exposing young dual language learners to English takes advantage of the brain's early language-learning openness. Still, remember that much of what a child knows has been stored in his brain in his home language. You may use a number of strategies to support his learning of English, but that doesn't mean he will know the same concepts in English if he first learned them in, say, a Spanish-speaking environment. For example, a child who has a pet cat at home will learn words and concepts about that cat—its care and habits—in her home language. If there are pet fish in the classroom, she may learn more about fish in English. The child might learn some related concepts, like eating and sleeping, in both languages, in both contexts. Other words and ideas may be picked up in one language but not yet transferred to the other language.

It is best not to turn language learning into a lesson. Just as we support a child's home language development by following her interests and engaging with her in exploring, repeating, and pretending, so we provide the same kinds of supports for the new language. Establishing communication skills is paramount in the first three years, as the child learns to get his needs met. Words add meaning to that communication as the child develops skills in one or more languages. Infant/toddler teachers need to share the experiences of the children in the here and now rather than preparing in advance activities or vocabulary lists.

> ## Demonstrate Interactive Reading
>
> Reading to infants and toddlers may not come naturally to all parents. They may not see the point in reading to children who do not yet talk. They may lack confidence in their own reading abilities. Or they may not know or remember how much fun active, interactive reading can be. Programs need to show parents how to read and tell stories with their young children. To make it easier for parents who don't speak your language, make a brief developmentally appropriate reading video to post on a site such as www.youtube.com or the program's website. Staff at The King's Daughters Day School provide a workshop to demonstrate to all parents how to read stories that capture their child's attention and build language skills.

Establish a classroom lending library of age-appropriate books—wordless, bilingual, or written in the families' languages.

Working Effectively With Diverse Families

Working with parents is one of the most important responsibilities of an infant/toddler teacher. When the parents don't speak your language, it is harder to build an effective partnership. As populations change and diversity grows in all areas of the country, strategies for overcoming this obstacle are vital for everyone who works with infants and toddlers. Strategies that help you interact with non-English-speaking parents also help improve your communication with all families.

Offer activities to involve diverse parents—think outside the box. The King's Daughters Day School offers families several options to participate, so the program can be responsive to families' schedules. Families may participate in planning the annual international festival, or they may bring some of their talents into the classroom, like writing Chinese characters for classroom labels.

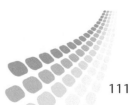

Involving parents in the program offers multiple benefits: (a) parents see teachers model interactions and activities that can benefit their child; (b) teachers see parents and children interact and can offer support as needed; (c) teachers can learn to use some of the same strategies that a child's family uses for approaching, comforting, caregiving, and interacting; and (d) parent involvement supports family strength and the parents' bond with the child—knowing and understanding what the child does all day helps parents feel confident and connected.

Some parents may prefer to help outside of the classroom—for example, making photocopies or cleaning toys or making furniture for the program. Offering options like these makes it more likely that you will find a way for every parent to get involved in the program and you will get to know those parents.

Another tip for bringing parents into the program is to offer them something they feel they need, such as English as a second language classes, cultural cooking groups, or workshops on applying for jobs. These types of services can be more effective than offering parents something *you* think they need, such as a workshop on parenting. If you offer parent workshops and rarely get enough parents to attend, it's time to broaden your thinking.

Create a family area. Create a welcoming area that encourages families to stop and sit a while, so they have time to talk to the teachers and each other. Some comfortable chairs, a pot of coffee and some cookies, and decorations related to the children's activities can create that kind of atmosphere. This may seem like a simple idea, but it actually is a very effective strategy in diverse programs because it encourages parents to slow down and get comfortable with the program, staff, and other families. Learning to communicate across language barriers takes a lot of time—time spent together—and plenty of opportunities to interact in pleasant, low-pressure situations to build the kind of rapport needed when you don't speak the same language as the family. Families rushing in and out to drop off or pick up their children, or families that only interact with staff during stressful times such as reminders about overdue bills or parent–teacher conferences, are less likely to overcome communication difficulties.

Support home literacy practices. This is one of infant/toddler teachers' most important strategies for involving parents in their children's learning! When programs do not have staff who speak the languages needed to read to all the children, it is particularly important to help families build home literacy practices. Establish a classroom lending library of age-appropriate books—wordless, bilingual, or written in the families' languages. Encourage families to bring in books in their home language to share. If the books are hard to find in the United States, families might obtain them during visits to or from relatives or on vacations. Two sources for books and materials in a variety of languages are www.languagelizard.com and www.chinasprout.com.

Handling Difficult Conversations Across a Language Barrier

A number of challenging topics may come up in parent–teacher meetings, so it is best to establish a positive rapport with families before the need arises for a difficult conversation. Developing a trusting relationship across a language barrier takes a bit of extra effort. Sharing pictures and videos of their child's activities and accomplishments can help you and the parents begin to bond. The more time you spend together, the easier it will be to understand each other and to use nonverbal cues effectively.

Have an interpreter on hand. Ideally, when the time comes for an important conversation, a certified interpreter should be present. When this is not possible, ask a trusted staff member or a member of the family to help. Sometimes it is tempting to use another child in the family to interpret. Unless there is an emergency and no other choice, avoid this option, because this may place undue pressure on the other child, who may not have the maturity or fluency to interpret complex information. Programs need to find qualified staff who are bilingual, even if such teachers are not in every room where children speak their language. When staff at The King's Daughters Day School encounter an unfamiliar language, they seek help from community organizations and agencies, such as the local child care resource and referral agency or nearby communities of faith, to ensure that they are doing everything possible to communicate effectively with every parent. Remind conference participants about confidentiality.

Plan ahead. Prepare a message board with key phrases in English and in the family's home language, so that you and the child's family members can point to the items you want to communicate. Photographs of the child that show examples of the behavior or situation that led to the conversation may help parents understand what you are trying to say about their child. Google Translate is an online tool that lets you type your message and hear it spoken in another language. However, a computerized translation system may use words that are more applicable to businesses or tourism and not technically accurate for an early childhood discussion, so do not depend on it for everything. Ask the parents for permission to record your meeting so you can ask an interpreter to clarify what was said, even if the interpreter cannot be present during the initial meeting. This also allows you to make additional notes about the conversation and to notice any areas that did not seem clear and need to be addressed further.

Sharing pictures and videos of their child's activities and accomplishments can help you and the parents begin to bond.

Be aware of personal or cultural issues. Keep in mind that there may be personal and/or cultural differences with regard to holding a parent–teacher meeting. Some cultures give less attention to on-time arrivals than others. Some parents may bring their whole family to a meeting with the teacher, and others may be so embarrassed that they won't even tell their family about the meeting. Do not assume that the parents will be comforted by a hug or by taking their hand. It is usually best to ask first.

Keep the message clear and brief. One of the hardest yet most effective strategies for holding conferences with parents who speak other languages is to say a lot less than you usually do. Prepare in advance by carefully reducing your messages to only the most critical and factual information. This makes it easier for translation and interpretation and more likely that the parents will come away with some real understanding. If you need to ask the family to do something, such as pick up their child earlier or take the child to the doctor or seek an evaluation, try to state that goal as simply and clearly as possible, then stick to a very few clear observations to explain your concerns.

Allow time to digest the information. Difficult messages are never easy to hear. They can be even more challenging for people who are not sure they understand everything you say and are not sure how to ask important questions. For these reasons, it may be best to plan the conversation over two meetings, allowing time for the family to absorb and think about the information. Then the parties can get back together to plan ways to resolve the issue. Keep in mind that a parent–teacher conference is a two-way conversation, not a lecture. Leave enough time for the parents to ask questions before asking them to take action.

Resolve differences based on language or cultural issues. As well as being culture based, some childrearing differences "may result from a family tradition, an individual experience, specific kinds of training, and philosophical ideals" (Gonzalez-Mena 2009). It is not essential that you know every cultural belief and practice for each group represented in your care. Rather, it is important that you get to know each family and what is important to them.

> A family enrolls their 2-year-old in an early childhood program. The director places him in the older toddler classroom, where he seems to adjust well. The mother spends several hours in the room with him on the first day. On the second day, and for a number of days thereafter, the mother leaves the child but returns at lunchtime to spoon feed him his entire meal.
>
> The teacher has a strong negative reaction to the child's being fed. She feels it is critical for a 2-year-old to practice self-help skills, and she voices her reservations to the parents. The parents stand their ground, explaining that in their culture, feeding a young child is a sign of love and caring.
>
> Over time, the teacher and parents learn to listen to each other. Everyone takes a step back and arrives at a compromise: the parents will gradually reduce the number of days a week they arrange to feed their son, and the teacher will help the family find activities that the child can use to develop self-help skills in other ways.

Focus on Infants and Toddlers

Conclusion

It may take practice to become comfortable with varied cultural and familial practices—especially the ones that seem counterproductive to you. A strong sense of self-awareness will help you detect whether you are really looking out for a child's best interests or whether you are just trying to make the family do things your way. Mutual respect between you and the children's families will help you know and understand them as individuals and as family units, including all the unique characteristics and cultural practices that make them who they are. Knowing the child, his interests, his family context, his culture, and his language is important in implementing developmentally appropriate practice.

Fort and Stechuk remind us that young children need support for their home language for social-emotional reasons as well as for cognitive reasons: "In a place where no one speaks the child's language and knows very little of his culture, a child could feel lost, misunderstood, and alienated" (2008, 24). Early care and education professionals can use developmentally appropriate practices that encompass a child's social and emotional needs in the context of facilitating the development of both English and the home language. According to Rebecca Parlakian, "Social-emotional skills are an integral part of school readiness because they give very young children the skills they need to communicate, cooperate, and cope in new environments" (2004, 39). Infant/toddler teachers can develop skills, learn strategies, and find resources that greatly enhance their success with diverse children and families. It may take extra work, but the benefits can last a lifetime.

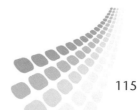

Learning to Be *Me* While Coming to Understand *We*: Encouraging Prosocial Babies in Group Settings

Mary Benson McMullen, Jennifer M. Addleman,
Amanda M. Fulford, Sarah L. Moore, Shari J. Mooney,
Samantha S. Sisk, and Jasmine Zachariah

At the same time young babies are developing an understanding of self as separate from others—what it means to be *me*—many also face having to negotiate living, learning, growing, and developing as part of a group—what it means to be *we*. This is true for more than half of all infants in the United States under the age of 9 months, who now spend many or most of their waking hours in some type of group care outside the home (Kreader, Ferguson, & Lawrence 2005; US Census Bureau 2013).

During a recent sabbatical from my university position, I (Mary McMullen) spent time in a number of early care and education classrooms with infants and toddlers, ages 3 months to 18 months, and their caregivers. I studied what life is like for babies in group settings. I tried to do this through the babies' eyes by looking at their day-to-day, lived experiences. In three classrooms I observed babies who showed higher levels of social competence than I had expected to see in children so young—much higher than what traditional child development theories tell us. I was equally impressed by the teachers who encouraged and supported these behaviors. These three classrooms are featured in this article.

Clearly something special was going on in these three rooms, something that allowed strong positive social-emotional development to occur in infants and toddlers and prosocial skills to flourish. I reflected on this, going back over the field notes from my study. I examined my photographs of babies and caregiving behaviors. I engaged in follow-up discussions with the lead teachers from each setting. I revisited some of the early literature written on this topic by well-known child development scholars (Erikson 1950; Kohlberg 1971; Piaget & Inhelder 1969; Vygotsky [1934]1986;) and then looked at the latest thinking about the roots of caring and early social skill development in very young children (Eisenberg 1992; Hyson 2004, Katz & McClellen 1997; Noddings 2003). This article is the result of my examinations, reflections, and discussions with the teachers, who are also the six coauthors of this article.

As you read our examples, look at the photographs, and reflect on our definition of babies' prosocial behavior, think about how often you see these behaviors among infants and toddlers in groups you encounter in your daily life and work. Consider how the caregiving and teaching practices you engage in or observe may encourage or discourage prosocial behavior in babies.

Consider how the caregiving and teaching practices you engage in or observe may encourage or discourage prosocial behavior in babies.

What Prosocial Babies Look Like

Many classic definitions of prosocial behavior are similar to Eisenberg's (1992), who describes it as "voluntary behavior intended to benefit another, such as helping, sharing, and comforting" (3). Some scholars stumble over the word *intended* when it concerns infants and toddlers, saying babies are incapable of being prosocial because even if they do something socially positive, it is unlikely to be altruistic (that is, deliberately selfless). The behaviors of the babies in these high-quality classrooms—friendship, sharing, caring, rule following, helpfulness, cooperation, and many others—may or may not satisfy the test for being truly altruistic, but they

Reaching out to interact with those around them is a positive outward social expression seen in prosocial babies.

were certainly *pro-* rather than *anti*social. Antisocial behavior involves showing disregard for others or being uncooperative or disagreeable. People who are antisocial are potentially destructive to themselves or the community.

We offer a different definition of prosocial behaviors, one that avoids notions of intention or motivation. We define prosocial behaviors for babies in a group setting as the communications and behaviors on the part of a baby that help create a positive emotional climate in the group and that involve reaching out—positive, discernable, outward social expression on the part of one baby toward one or more other individuals, whether infant or adult.

In group care, as in life in general, we teachers tend to place a premium on prosocial behaviors and make it a priority to help children acquire those skills and characteristics (see "Prosocial Skills and Related Attributes," p. 118). And now, with our youngest babies more frequently being placed in

Being prosocial starts with babies understanding who they are as individuals and feeling valued for the unique people they are.

group care, the important life lessons about group and community living begin very early.

Caregivers and teachers who care for the youngest children play a powerful role, alongside families, in contributing to the emotional well-being and social development of babies; their impact may lead to positive—or negative—long-term outcomes for children. "We tend to go through life feeling the way our attachment persons made us feel—be that happy or in turmoil," says Honig (2002, 6). Research connects strong, secure, relationship-based early practices with young children to positive long-term cognitive, social, and mental health

outcomes in older children and adults (NRC 2001; Ramey & Ramey 1999; Shonkoff & Phillips 2000; Shore 1997).

Prosocial Babies Are Cared For and Respected as Individuals

For babies to become prosocial, they must first and foremost be cared for by caring adults. In the relationship captured in the photo below, the baby has the caregiver's undivided attention and the caregiver responds in a loving manner. In moments of mindful, respectful, sensitively responsive caregiving like this, babies receive messages and lessons about what it means to be responded to with kindness and compassion, and this is at the heart of learning about empathy (Eisenberg 1992; Noddings 2003).

In a recent conference presentation, DaRos-Voseles (2009) said, "Children who come from caring homes come to school with that expectation; others come with that need." Regardless of which babies come to us in our classrooms, we need to give them countless opportunities to experience the reciprocal, reflexive nature of being in a caring relationship, so they can learn the give-and-take, back-and-forth of being part of such relationships.

We also need to respect all babies as individuals. Very early on, babies begin to understand themselves as separate individuals in their own right, different and apart from others. They have their own personal characteristics and preferences, temperaments and needs (Field 2007), and they need to feel that their caregivers value and respect those traits (Abbott & Langston 2005).

> We don't view babies as lesser beings, but as full, capable human beings, deserving of our respect.
>
> **(Teacher Comment)**

Self-confidence—trusting in one's own abilities and what one can do—is also critical in being able to reach out to others in a caring manner. A baby becomes confident through close, supportive relationships and having plenty of opportunities to explore and try new things. Babies need opportunities to make things move and spin and rattle and make noise, and they are so pleased when they can do things by themselves or with minimal support or intervention. Most of all, however, they want the people they care about to notice what they do and to respond.

Being in a caring relationship is rewarding for both participants.

We try to make the children feel special and unique by providing interesting activities that are challenging but achievable for each and every one of them. We provide the support and encouragement needed for them to complete the tasks and gain a sense of pride. We put mirrors around the room so they can see themselves playing, and we communicate to them how special we think they are by giving them lots of hugs throughout the day.

(Teacher Comment)

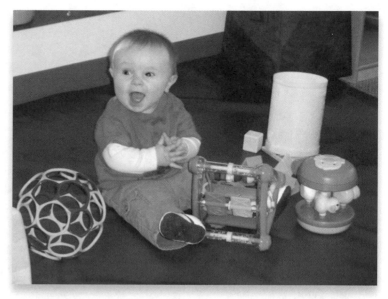

Prosocial Babies Are Friendly and Kind to Others

Peer interaction occurs in babies as young as 3 months, and researchers report clear friendship preferences among young infants and toddlers (Riley et al. 2008). Being able to form friendships is very important in the overall healthy growth and development of very young children (Katz & McClellan 1997; Riley et al. 2008). Children with friends are found to be happier, better at working out social difficulties, and generally more competent (Brazelton & Greenspan 2000). Riley and colleagues (2008) argue that the experience of caring about other individuals that occurs through friendship is how children's early peer interactions become truly prosocial: "Within a friendship children can develop altruistic values, that is, prosocial behavior motivated by concern for others rather than the expectation of personal reward" (45–46).

Prosocial babies love to make things happen on their own, but they feel especially pleased when those they care about notice.

The caregivers and teachers of the infants and toddlers in these rooms addressed the babies as *friends*. Babies notice each other and even show clear friendship preferences very early, as premobile infants. They frequently take special delight

Two buddies spot each other, crawl toward one another, and greet each other warmly— "High five!"

when their buddies arrive in the morning and miss them when they are absent. The prosocial babies in these groups seek out their special buddies for play.

In our room we have two boys, Hans and Hou Hou, who are clearly best friends. When one is already in the room and the other one arrives, the first one stops whatever he's doing to run to greet the other. They squeal in delight and run off, and typically start a game of chase or just laugh and laugh and imitate each other for the longest time.

(Teacher Comment)

Prosocial babies frequently show affection for one another with hugs, kisses, pats, and snuggles.

Older infants play contentedly alongside younger infants, often reinforced by the caregiver's words reminding them, "Gentle, please; gentle touch."

It is also common for the prosocial babies in these classrooms to show affection for one another and for their caregivers, occasionally offering pats, hugs, and kisses. Their caregivers freely snuggle, cuddle, and hug the babies. Such behavior, which fosters closeness and warmth in caregiving relationships, is a key element in encouraging prosocial development in very young children (Honig 2002).

I believe strongly that an infant's ability to be prosocial begins at birth and is continually fostered by the way the caregiver develops a loving, warm, and supportive relationship with the infant. Babies are delighted just to be with their friends and with their caregiver. When I was reading *Brown Bear Brown Bear, What Do You See?* little Norah crawled right up close to me, pulled herself up, gave me a hug, and made herself comfortable in the center of my lap.

(Teacher Comment)

Also notable in these groups is that babies of different ages play peacefully and contentedly side by side, older infants with younger, premobile infants. It is even typical to see babies sharing toys.

Quann and Wien (2006) define empathy in young children as "the capacity to observe the feelings of another and to respond with care and concern for that other" (22). Learning to value and appreciate others is the root of empathy. We saw many infant and toddler behaviors that fit this definition of empathy, or what we considered to be kindness. Babies in these rooms regularly comforted one another when they were sad, frightened, or injured. Older babies acted with care and caution around younger premobile infants—for instance, handing them toys that were out of reach or giving them pacifiers they had lost. Some behaviors were even more remarkable:

Focus on Infants and Toddlers

> We were playing in the large-motor room, and Rosie needed her nose wiped. We noticed this because Matilda walked over to the box of tissues and took one out, walked over to Rosie, and rubbed her face with the tissue, making a smeary mess all over her face! She then walked over to the trash can and put [the tissue] in the trash and went back and continued to play. We teachers stood and watched in amazement.
>
> **(Teacher Comment)**

Empathy in infants and toddlers may sometimes take the form of caregiving behavior, as with Matilda. Babies appear to be modeling something they have seen or been on the receiving end of many times. But sometimes the actions seem to go even further, indicating that they are internalizing a strong moral sense—with ideas about what they think is right or fair. Consider the actions of baby Faridah:

> Little Faridah seems to have appointed herself the "mommy police." We have a mom that comes at lunch to breastfeed her infant son, and sometimes he falls asleep just before she arrives. Faridah often sits and plays near his crib, waiting for him to wake up, keeping her eye on him. If, while waiting, the mom picks up another baby, Faridah gestures at the crib and the mom, and squeals with a tone that indicates she is correcting the parent.
>
> **(Teacher Comment)**

Prosocial Babies Feel a Sense of Belonging to Their Community

"Children need to be where they feel that they belong" (Jennings 2005, 92–93). Babies thrive when they are with familiar and trusted friends and adult caregivers, where they feel welcomed and accepted (Abbott & Langston 2005). In the group care of young babies, this is accomplished best in smaller groups with a consistent primary caregiver. In such groups, babies learn how to be increasingly social. Engaging in activities together, such as taking walks and stroller rides, reading, participating in short circle or group times, and having highly social mealtimes, all foster a sense of belonging and give babies opportunities to practice social skills.

> We build community throughout the day, but mainly through activities such as music time, when we sing and get all excited about our friends who came to the room today. Also, I have started making classroom books filled with pictures of the children and staff, and a "stroller walk" book with pictures of people, places, and objects we see on our walks.
>
> **(Teacher Comment)**

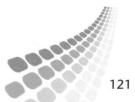

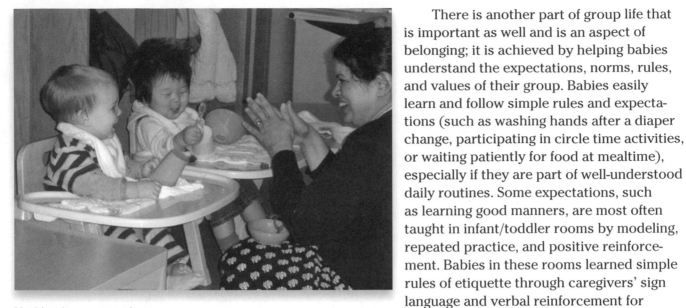

There is another part of group life that is important as well and is an aspect of belonging; it is achieved by helping babies understand the expectations, norms, rules, and values of their group. Babies easily learn and follow simple rules and expectations (such as washing hands after a diaper change, participating in circle time activities, or waiting patiently for food at mealtime), especially if they are part of well-understood daily routines. Some expectations, such as learning good manners, are most often taught in infant/toddler rooms by modeling, repeated practice, and positive reinforcement. Babies in these rooms learned simple rules of etiquette through caregivers' sign language and verbal reinforcement for responses such as please and thank you.

Mealtime is an opportunity to foster community and belonging to the group.

Caregivers explicitly teach other rules, again through positive reinforcement and plenty of practice and patience. These are rules about doing what is expected at cleanup time, going up the stairs of the climber and down the slide, and playing away from the area where babies are sleeping. Caregivers positively and respectfully transmitted the messages about behaviors expected in the group, in the classroom, and in society as a whole. They taught the babies respect for self, for property, and for others. Babies easily seemed to understand that "these are things I should do" and "these are things I should not do when I am in this group outside of my home and family."

Some rules of group life have to be taught explicitly, such as those about health and safety, like hand washing, and rules about fairness, like taking turns going up the climber stairs, one at a time.

Talking constantly with the babies and telling them what's going on and what we are doing is yet another way of respecting them and communicating expectations. It is truly surprising how much even the young babies understand. Another related strategy is singing. We try to instill a feeling of belonging to the group by singing songs and nursery rhymes together, especially songs with the babies' names in them. Also we repeatedly talk and sign with actions the words for please and thank you, and we give a lot of love to each baby when teaching these ideas.

(Teacher Comment)

Focus on Infants and Toddlers

Prosocial babies love to be helpful in the care-giving environment. Give a toddler a small broom and dustpan or a sponge and just stand back and watch him work! Of course, helping sometimes does not extend to doing so at the scheduled, routine cleanup times, as we probably all have experienced. This, however, seems to show a child's reluctance to quit doing something highly valued and move on to a teacher-selected activity, like putting things away. The teachers in these rooms moved the babies and toddlers into free play, cleanup, and other activities with transition songs and rhymes (see "Simple Transition Songs") and by giving them verbal cues, such as, "Friends, in three minutes I'm going to set up for snack."

> ## Simple Transition Songs
>
> Clean up, clean up,
> Everybody, everywhere.
> Clean up, clean up,
> Everybody do their share.
>
> Come follow, follow, follow,
> Come follow, follow, me.
> Come follow, follow, follow.
> The Big Room's where I'll be.

Discussion

Clearly, adults should never underestimate the competence of young children. I am reminded of this whenever I spend a significant amount of time in early care and education settings. In the case of these three classrooms, it was evident that infants and toddlers were indeed up to the challenge of grappling with understanding the difficult lessons of becoming *we* and *me* at the same time. As seen in this article and others (Eisenberg 1992; Quann & Wien 2006), young babies have a remarkable capacity for prosocial behavior, an ability greatly underestimated by traditional child development theorists.

My experience in studying infants and toddlers in group settings also taught me that not all young babies in group care demonstrate this capacity for behaving prosocially. That is to say, not all babies have the opportunity to do so. I did not see it in most of the other rooms in which I observed. The three classrooms had several characteristics in common that the others did not. They were part of early childhood programs that met or exceeded the standards and criteria for earning NAEYC Accreditation of Programs for Young Children. The teachers were all professionally trained and highly experienced in teaching and caring for this young age group, and their practices reflected their belief in the importance of relationships and developmentally appropriate care and learning (Copple & Bredekamp 2009; McMullen 1999; McMullen & Dixon 2006, 2009). My research did not look specifically at the relationship of the beliefs and practices of caregivers that encourage versus discourage early prosocial behaviors in infants and toddlers, and therefore I cannot draw conclusions with confidence. But I invite others to investigate this issue further.

Can we conclude that the behaviors I saw were truly prosocial, by the strict definition that includes being altruistic? Eisenberg (1992) and Quann and Wien (2006) indicate that chief among a baby's motivations for prosocial behavior may be to please their teachers, to get social approval from a peer or the group, or to accomplish something for an external reward (for example, to get something they want or to do something they want to do). But at this age, behavior motivation is probably not what really matters in a prosocial baby.

We believe that whether truly prosocial or not, these behaviors put the babies well on their way to having what they need to get along well as social beings.

This article was first published in the July 2009 issue of *Young Children*.

Mary Benson McMullen, PhD, is professor of early childhood education at Indiana University in Bloomington. Her current research focuses on fostering physical and psychological well-being through relationship-based practices in children birth to age 3.

Jennifer M. Addleman, BA, was colead teacher in the infant/toddler room at Indiana University's Campus View Child Care Center in Bloomington at the time of this study.

Amanda M. Fulford is an early childhood educator in Bloomington, Indiana.

Sarah L. Moore, BS, is an infant/toddler specialist at The Child Care Resource Network in Lafayette, Indiana.

Shari J. Mooney is the head teacher of the multiage infant/toddler classroom at the Ben and Maxine Miller Child Development Laboratory School at Purdue University, in West Lafayette, Indiana.

Samantha S. Sisk has worked as an infant/toddler teacher at Indiana University's Early Childhood Education Services at Campus View Child Care Center for 10 years, and is currently completing her MEd.

Jasmine Zachariah, MS, is a coteacher in the infant/toddler room at Indiana University's Campus Children's Center.

The prosocial babies I observed lived up to the definition of helping "to create a positive emotional climate in the group" and of "reaching out with positive social expressions . . . toward one or more others." We see these behaviors as good for the overall group, whatever the reasons for them. Further, the behaviors may become a pattern for the way an individual baby lives, and in doing so, may become internalized and part of the baby's code of behavior, their moral code (Brazelton & Greenspan 2000). Thus, we believe that whether truly prosocial or not, these behaviors put the babies well on their way to having what they need to get along well as social beings.

The teachers in these rooms naturally behaved in the manner they expected of all members of their classroom communities. They showed respect to everyone in the room—to each other as colleagues, to parents and families, and most important of all, to the babies. In my research journal, an entry about one of the teachers speaks to the kind of respectful caregiving I saw in these rooms:

> Her wonderful gentle manner, the way she speaks to the babies, how they are all her friends . . . how she sets up the room. . . . Only someone who utterly respects and values babies could put that kind of effort into this the way she does, almost like she is setting a beautiful table for honored guests, each and every morning.

Final Thoughts

Caring, friendship, kindness, affection, empathy, belonging, following rules, meeting norms and expectations, adopting the values of our culture and our society—all of these are lessons for life to be learned along the way. They usually are acquired later in childhood. As I observed the amazing babies in these rooms and the remarkable teachers in my study, I found myself recalling the words of essayist Robert Fulghum ([1986] 2004) in his well-known piece *All I Really Need to Know I Learned in Kindergarten*.

Infant care is part of everyday life for most babies, and their early caregivers can have a tremendous and enduring effect on their well-being, development, and future functioning. It seems that the truly important and enduring life lessons about who we are, how we get along with others, and how to be the best people we can be begin in the infant/toddler care and education environment—or rather, in the *high-quality* infant/toddler care and education environment.

What Do We Mean by Reading Readiness?

Nikki Darling-Kuria

For the last several days, Janet had been anxious about her upcoming parent–teacher conference with Sam, 18-month-old Abby's father. Sam had recently brought in alphabet flash cards because he wants Abby to learn to read. Janet completely understood Sam's desire to support his daughter's early language skills, but she was not comfortable with the method or the timing.

Janet brought her concerns to the director, Maria. "How can I help Sam understand that before Abby can read, she needs to have the strong foundational skills that come before letter recognition? You know we work on those skills every day. We tell stories, we talk to the children in ways that introduce them to new words and more complex use of language, and we read aloud from books and printed pages so they get the connection between words on a page and spoken language. Our training has taught us that flash cards for children so young are not effective in building toddlers' language skills. Their brains are not ready for rote memorization. But how do I say that to Sam so I support his interest without sounding critical?"

Maria understood the dilemma. She had been feeling the same pressure from other parents at the center. She said, "Have you asked Sam why he wants Abby to learn her ABCs now? Maybe the conference can be a time for you to hear about his hopes and goals for Abby. Then you can connect to those goals and share what you know about early language and literacy development. You can help him see that you and he are partners in supporting Abby's language learning. One resource you could share with him is the new parent guide the state just published, the one that goes along with the state infant and toddler early learning guidelines you use in the toddler room."

Janet read the parent guide and decided to begin the conference by asking about Sam's goals and expectations for Abby, as Maria suggested. It crossed her mind that Sam was probably using the best technique he knew of with the flash cards. If he was interested in discussing early language development and understanding how to support it, she would share the guide and explain the practices she uses with the children and connect those to emerging language skills.

Some families, wanting what is best for their children, believe that being able to read as early as possible is the best predictor of academic success later. After all, there is a constant bombardment of product advertisements promising that *any* child *any* age can become the next Einstein if only the right combination of expensive toys and DVDs are purchased. It's easy to get caught up in the promises that new, better products will make smarter children. No wonder Janet and Sam have different ideas about what will work best!

Janet needs Sam's help in understanding his perspective, and Sam needs help in interpreting his observations about Abby's emerging language skills. Janet wants to establish a partnership with Sam that will benefit Abby's devel-

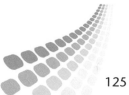

opment. Her plan is to listen to and respond to Sam and share her knowledge about early development with him so that they can come to an agreement about what each can do to support Abby's emerging language skills.

Janet reflected on a recent infant brain development workshop she had attended to help her identify some talking points for the conference with Sam. Janet had learned that memorizing is often mistaken as learning. In fact, rote memorization is a lower level skill compared to skills developed through complex language use, which emerges in the context of meaningful relationships that motivate communication of thoughts and feelings (Hirsh-Pasek, Golinkoff, & Eyer 2003). She knows that a great way to encourage Abby to talk is to pay attention to her and to what she is doing, making comments that connect to her experience. For example:

> "Abby, I see you ate all your chicken. Chicken is good for you and will help you grow big and STRONG (*arms out, flexing muscles*)!"

Janet plans to suggest that she and Abby's father both can keep this narration running throughout the day. They can describe a variety of emotions, like surprise, excitement, or sadness, as appropriate. Working together, they can give Abby the context she needs to make sense of all the new words she hears. For example, Sam can repeat the words Abby uses or use words in place of her gestures.

> Abby points to the cracker box and says "cra."
> Sam asks, "Would Abby like some crackers (*handing Abby the crackers*)? Are these the crackers that Abby wants?"

Sam can help give Abby her words until she is ready to do it herself by modeling a rich vocabulary in the context of their everyday lives.

The infant and toddler early learning guidelines, which explain what infants know and can do at various stages, provides Janet with further information to share about how toddlers develop and learn. Here is a sample of what she read about language and literacy for 18-month-olds. Children between the ages of 18 and 24 months are starting to "recognize and react to the sounds of language" (MSDE & HUSE 2010, 21). That is why toddlers start paying attention to rhymes in songs and identifying sounds different animals make. Recognizing that a cow says "moo" and a dog says "ruff, ruff" is learning in context.

Another guideline states that children 18 to 24 months "begin to develop imitative reading"; for example, a child "might fill in words in a familiar text" (MSDE & JHUSE 2010, 21). Janet has noticed, and will share with Sam, that Abby finishes the phrases in a familiar book that is read to her. This is very exciting and shows that Abby's language capacities are developing as expected for a child her age. Such seemingly simple activities build connections in Abby's brain and help her develop the skills she will need to communicate and help her when she is ready to read.

After deciding on an approach that will establish her respect for Sam's concerns and reflecting on her own understanding of infant language development, Janet felt better prepared for their conference. She was looking forward to hearing Sam's thoughts and sharing her learning. She was confident that

This article was first published in the January 2012 issue of *Young Children* in the column Rocking and Rolling: Supporting Infants, Toddlers, and Their Families.

Nikki Darling-Kuria, MA, is a senior writer/training specialist with ZERO TO THREE.

together she and Sam could come up with realistic goals for Abby that centered on her developing early reading skills that would last a lifetime.

Think About It

- What are your beliefs about helping children become good communicators and readers?

- How do you go about building partnerships with families? Why is this important?

- What are some of the ways you share your practices with families? What are some early literacy and communication strategies you learned from families?

Try It

- Develop some conversation starters that demonstrate your interest in partnering with families.

- Research your state's infant and toddler early learning guidelines. If your state doesn't have infant and toddler early learning guidelines, then use *Healthy Beginnings: Supporting Development and Learning From Birth Through Three Years of Age* (MSDE & JHUSE 2010), which you can access online at http://cte.jhu.edu/onlinecourses/HealthyBeginnings/HBFINAL.pdf.

- Create a book about the child's day that families can share at home with their child. Ask families to create a book about their child's day at home that you can share in your program.

- Create some talking points that share your knowledge about supporting emergent literacy in very young children. Practice with a colleague or mentor ways you might begin the conversations. For example:

  "Sam, I know how deeply you care about Abby's development. You really spend a lot of time with her in activities that you both enjoy. I appreciate the books you have brought in to share with the class, and I will use them. If you have any favorite rhyming songs that you sing at home, I would love to hear about them. I think that as we both continue to enjoy talking to Abby and reading and singing with her, she naturally will start talking more and learn more words. You will be amazed how quickly that happens. She will be eager and excited to learn to read when she's a little older."

Rocking and Rolling is written by infant/toddler specialists and contributed to *Young Children* by ZERO TO THREE, a nonprofit organization working to promote the health and development of infants and toddlers by translating research and knowledge into a range of practical tools and resources for use by the adults who influence the lives of young children.

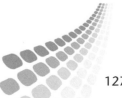

Using Toys to Support Infant–Toddler Learning and Development

Gabriel Guyton

Colorful scarves fill the air in a mixed-age, inclusive infant and toddler class-room. Most of the young children dance and move, swaying their bodies and hands while waving their scarves. Maggie is 2½ years old, but her play and skills are more typical of a younger child. Instead of dancing with the others, she sits alone, happily mouthing a few scarves. Her teacher, Vicky, wants to help Maggie expand her play. Vicky understands where Maggie is developmentally and also knows Maggie enjoys filling and dumping. The teacher stuffs scarves inside an empty tissue box, leaving a small piece poking out. Maggie excitedly pulls scarves from the box and laughs; a new game is born. By being aware of Maggie's developmental skills and interests, Vicky has used a simple toy to facilitate the toddler's cognitive development through play.

Choosing toys and activities that are suitable for infants and toddlers can challenge even the most experienced teacher. By being mindful of the basic principles of child development and the role of play, teachers can intentionally select toys to meet young children's unique needs and interests, supporting learning. It is also important to be aware of the essential role of teacher–child interactions. When teachers engage with children as they play, teachers help children make sense of their experiences and promote children's further exploration (Johnson & Johnson 2006).

Understanding Development and Toys

Play is the mechanism by which children learn—how they experience their world, practice new skills, and internalize new ideas—and is therefore the essential "work of children" (Paley 2004). Through this continuous and expanding process, early skills give rise to new ones and new experiences are integrated with previous ones. Through play, children learn about the world and engage in activities that encourage their cognitive, emotional, and social development (Elkind 2007). For example, when a child bangs on a drum, she learns she can create a sound. Through play, she learns the important concept of cause and effect.

Teachers can build on children's play by providing engaging toys. Effective toys are safe and suited to the child's age, abilities, and interests. When a child expresses an interest in animals, for example, a teacher can build on this by adding animal toys to block play. Block play provides a foundation for learning about problem solving and basic math and science concepts.

Child development occurs across several domains, including language, fine motor, gross motor, social-emotional, and cognitive development. When choosing materials and planning learning activities for children, teachers can

> By being mindful of the basic principles of child development and the role of play, teachers can intentionally select toys to meet young children's unique needs and interests, supporting learning.

consider how the toys and experiences will support development within and across these domains. Certain toys promote behaviors that encourage development within certain domains. For example, teachers can nurture the cognitive skill of object permanence by hiding a toy under a scarf and playing the classic peekaboo game.

A child's cognitive development involves thinking skills—the ability to process information to understand how the world works. Toys and play naturally provide opportunities for practicing different thinking skills, such as imitation, cause and effect, problem solving, and symbolic thinking. When a teacher models drumming on pots and pans, a child imitates and quickly learns to make a noise of his own. Offering this opportunity to play allows the child to practice imitation, to experience cause and effect, and to have fun discovering how the world works.

This article was first published in the September 2011 issue of *Young Children*.

Gabriel Guyton, MPsy, MEd, works at the Bank Street Family Center in New York, where she is head teacher in a mixed-age inclusion infant/toddler classroom, and also supervises student teachers.

Homemade Toys and Readily Available Materials

Many advertisements lead consumers to think that toys are better if they are expensive, store-bought items. In reality, the best toys are those selected based on their appropriateness for a child's age, development, and interests. Engaging toys are often homemade or readily available items such as fabric, bottles, cardboard boxes, yarn, cooking pans, pinecones—the options are practically limitless. This is especially important to keep in mind for economically challenged communities or just plain busy people. Even for people with the time and resources, making toys can be a more personal way to build relationships between teachers and children. Using photos of family members to make stick puppets, for example, is a wonderful way to bring the child's home into the classroom.

When choosing materials for toys, it is important to consider the children's communities and cultures. Teachers can bring into the classroom elements of different languages, dress, and music. When choosing or making books, for example, some can reflect the cultures and languages of the children. Similarly, dolls, dress-up clothes, and pretend food should represent children's families and communities.

A little creativity combined with basic materials can stimulate play and facilitate a young child's development across all domains (including cognitive). For example, teachers can use cardboard boxes, plastic dishes, pie tins, and sock puppets. In the following section, all of the suggested toys and materials can be handmade using easily acquired or inexpensive materials.

Thinking About Safety

When selecting toys, it is critical to consider the numerous safety issues specific to different developmental stages. Choking and falling are two concerns for infants and toddlers. Children love to move, and young children learning to control their bodies often fall or bump into things. Toys and other classroom materials should not have sharp edges or projections. Infants and toddlers often explore their world by putting things in their mouths. Small buttons or pieces that come off easily are choking hazards and should be avoided. Watch out for chipping paint, and select toys that are not toxic.

Be on the lookout for materials treated with potentially harmful substances, such as arsenic (used to treat some wood products), lead paint, and chemicals such as bisphenol A (BPA) and phthalates. Children's brains and bodies are smaller than adults' and are developing fast, making them especially vulnerable to toxic substances, even in small amounts. Look for labels on toys and materials (such as "nontoxic" or "BPA-free"), and check online resources such as www.gogreenratingscale.org.

Choosing and Using Toys to Support Cognitive Development

Teachers should be intentional about the toys they offer to children, regardless of whether they are homemade or store-bought. For example, many toddlers enjoy using modeling materials and props such as playdough. Offer it to children with some specific developmental goals in mind. Provide matching plastic cookie cutters, allowing children to make shapes and experience the ideas of "same" and "different" as they explore.

The following examples illustrate toys that are easy to find or make, as well as specific areas of cognitive development that can be addressed with the toys. Keep in mind that a lot of toys are open-ended—appropriate for children at different ages and developmental levels. Children can use these toys in many different ways, and they will hopefully spark your imagination to make other fun, educational toys for infant and toddler classrooms (see "Toys and Activities to Nurture Children's Cognitive Development, p. 132," for more ideas).

Fabric

Scarves and pieces of cloth of different colors and textures can come from old clothes, sheets, or fabric scraps provided by families, collected by teachers, or donated by a store in the community. Teachers can use fabric with children of all ages. A scarf can be a costume in dramatic play, an item to throw and catch, or something to put in a box and pull out again.

Example. Kaori, age 8 months, plays with her teacher, Devora, who hides a doll under a scarf and calls out, "Dolly, where are you?" Devora checks with Kaori, then lifts the scarf and says, "There you are, Dolly—peekaboo!" Kaori laughs, excited at the "return" of her doll.

Cognitive connection. Kaori is becoming aware of *object permanence*—the knowledge that an object is there even when it cannot be seen (Cole, Cole, & Lightfoot 2005). This is an essential step in an infant's cognitive development because understanding object permanence leads to an understanding of her world and an awareness that will allow her to learn, imitate, and explore. Through exploration of the environment and peekaboo and other games that involve hiding objects, a teacher can support children's emerging awareness of the environment around them (Brazelton & Sparrow 2006).

Blocks

Blocks are great toys for children of all ages. Blocks made of wood are one option, but teachers can also offer shoeboxes, cereal boxes, plastic bowls, cups, and paper bags filled with crumpled newspaper and taped shut. These simple blocks are best for children ages 2 years and under, while wooden unit blocks are good for ages 2 and up (MacDonald 2001). Children can explore, move, and hold blocks before beginning to stack them vertically or line them up horizontally to form simple structures or complex designs. They can select blocks of the same size or in uniformly descending sizes.

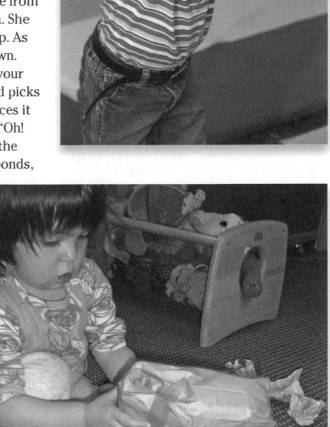

Example. Fatima, age 22 months, takes blocks made from cardboard boxes from an assorted pile in the block area. She stacks one on top of the other while playing at a tabletop. As she places a fourth block on top of her tower, it falls down. Fatima's teacher Maria says, "Look, the block is beside your foot." Fatima stops and looks to the side of her body and picks up the block. Fatima then picks up a large block and places it on a small block. The large block falls over. Maria says, "Oh! The big block fell off the small block." Fatima then puts the small block on top of the big block. Maria excitedly responds, "Look, you put the small block on top of the big block and it did not fall."

Cognitive connection. Fatima is gaining an understanding of spatial relationships—the ability to understand dimensions and shapes and how they work together. She is learning how to balance and fit pieces to build towers. As she expands this play through experience, she might build more complex structures, such as bridges and enclosures (MacDonald 2001).

Puzzles

A muffin pan accompanied by a variety of small objects can be an excellent first puzzle for infants and toddlers. Offer items that fit easily inside or, to make it more complicated, just barely fit. A muffin pan puzzle allows children to feel a sense of success since all the cups are the same size. To make puzzles that offer greater challenges, cut out circles or squares of different sizes in the top of a shoebox. Offer objects such as large recycled plastic jar tops, toy cars, or clothespins that just fit inside the cutouts.

Teachers can build on children's developing cognitive skills by creating simple picture puzzles. To make puzzles, draw a picture, print a photograph,

Toys and Activities to Nurture Children's Cognitive Development

Toy	Age (months)	Activity	Cognitive Connections
Mobile	0–6	Moving objects attract a young child's attention and stimulate interaction. Attach safe objects (such as pictures or large pinecones) to a string and hang the mobile so that a child can watch it move and also reach out and pull or bat items. The child can be lying on her back or sitting and reaching forward.	— Cause and effect — Sound and texture discoveries — Hand-eye coordination
Bottle with floating objects	6–9	Infants need toys that illustrate cause and effect. Fill a clear plastic baby bottle or soda bottle with water and add shells, rocks, floating glitter, or any object that captures a child's interest. Make sure the top is attached securely and, especially in a mixed-age room, preferably glued with all-purpose nontoxic glue. Children can shake the bottle to hear and see items move inside and roll it, which encourages crawlers to chase after it.	— Cause and effect — Intentionality
Knock-knock	9–12	Any "surprise" item that can be uncovered provides opportunities for children to discover and name. On a large piece of paper, draw or glue pictures. For each, cut out rectangles from different color paper that is large enough to hide the pictures. Attach these by gluing or taping down one long side so that they can be "opened" like doors. Have children knock on the doors and open them to reveal the hidden items.	— Object permanence — Cause and effect — Naming
Books	12–18	Early books are an excellent (and fun!) way for children to discover and name objects, and learn that pictures represent real things. Thin paper books can be difficult for very young children to manipulate. They also tear easily. Glue pictures of animals, everyday objects, or drawings onto pieces of thick cardboard, and bind the pages with glue or yarn. For a more interactive experience, glue pictures on fabric or papers of different textures.	— Early literacy — Language and vocabulary — Prediction — *Wh* questions (who, what, when, where, why)
I Spy telescope	18–24	Almost anything that is open on two ends can become a child's telescope. Use paper towel tubes, empty cracker boxes, or just roll a few sheets of paper and tape them together. Children can look through the telescope for things around the room or yard. Offer variations by asking children to look for specific items, colors, or categories. For example, "Do you see anything green? Do you see any animals?"	— Classification — Recognition — Language and vocabulary — Joint attention — Perspective taking
Puppets	24–36	Children can use puppets to tell stories and act out ideas. Make hand puppets from a variety of materials (such as paper, socks, cloth, and so on) or make a handheld puppet by gluing a picture to a stick. Decoration brings a puppet to life. For example, draw a face with markers, glue on pictures from a magazine, or adorn puppets with string or yarn.	— Imagination — Abstract thinking — Language — Sequencing

or cut out a picture from a magazine. Glue the picture to a piece of cardboard or paper plate so that the puzzle is easier to manipulate, and cut it into pieces that a child can reassemble.

Example. Raj, age 12 months, sits surrounded by objects of different sizes and shapes, including a plastic cup, a toy boat, and jar lids. His teacher places a muffin pan in front of him. Raj picks up objects and puts them in and out of the cup shapes in the pan, rotating pieces to make them fit. He concentrates with each new object and claps his hands in delight with each success.

Cognitive connection. As he manipulates objects to make them fit into the muffin pan, Raj is thinking and problem solving. As children are exposed to these types of activities, they learn to develop solutions, which boosts their confidence in their ability to solve problems. Without the frustration of precise puzzle pieces, early versions allow infants and toddlers to explore different sizes and shapes, and gain understanding of size dimensions and concepts of *in* and *out*. As children get older, teachers can introduce simple puzzles with a few pieces.

Rattles

Infants love making noise. Teachers can use a clean plastic container, small enough for a child to hold in one hand, to quickly make a wonderful noise-making toy. Fill the container with objects too large to be a choking hazard, such as shells or large bells. Make sure there is enough space for the objects to move freely inside. Seal the top with a lid using heavy tape.

Example. Mario, age 8 months, sits on the floor holding a small plastic water bottle partly filled with broken pieces of crayon. Music plays and Rosemary leans toward Mario, moving his hands up and down, singing, "Shake your maracas . . . shake, shake, shake your maracas." Mario smiles and imitates his teacher, shaking the bottle. Each time he moves the bottle, it makes more sound, encouraging him to keep up the motion.

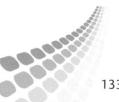

Cognitive connection. Mario is interested in activities that demonstrate cause and effect. Activities such as simple musical instruments offer children a chance to figure out how objects work and to connect their own actions with outcomes. This can lead to a greater sense of self-awareness and increased control over their environments.

Summary

Infants and toddlers engage in certain types of play, depending on their stage of development. Teachers can maximize opportunities to build new skills by being mindful of where children are developmentally, what their interests are, and what skills they, as educators, want children to explore. When teachers are aware of how specific cognitive skills can be practiced through play, they can choose toys and activities intentionally. As the underlying reasons for selecting specific toys and activities become clearer, a world of limitless possibilities for invented toys opens up.

As the primary vehicle for early childhood education, toys are an essential classroom ingredient. Teachers can easily make toys from inexpensive materials found in most communities. Readily available materials, when used appropriately, can stimulate play and development across all domains. While toys are important instruments in facilitating a child's development, above all, toys should be considered tools with which teachers can engage children.

Why Do Babies Like Boxes Best?

Linda Gillespie

It is Ella's first birthday, and her mother is excited. She places a present wrapped with bright paper in front of Ella and tears just a small portion of the paper. Ella takes over, pulling on the paper and scrunching it in her hands. Some tape gets stuck on her finger, and she pulls at it; then it gets stuck on another finger, and she pulls at that. With help, Ella eventually tears all the paper off the box.

Ella's mother opens the box and takes out the musical elephant inside. She shows Ella how, when she squeezes its foot, the elephant sings the ABC song! Ella looks at the elephant, then at the box and paper. She grabs the paper and crumples it, stuffs it into the box, turns the box upside down, and lets the paper fall out. Ella is delighted, and she does it again and again. In the meantime, Mom is squeezing the elephant's feet, trying to interest Ella in the real toy!

Wow, what happened here? Why does Ella prefer the wrapping paper and the box to the fancy toy inside? The answer lies in Ella's development. The toy in the box is one-dimensional, and while really cute and interesting to adults, it does not offer the endless opportunities that the box and the paper do for exploring with all the senses. Infants at one year of age are in the stage of development Piaget called sensorimotor play. The sensorimotor stage of play is characterized by babies actively exploring objects in their environment—first with their eyes, then with their hands and mouths. Ella spent her first year of life practicing this exploratory play.

In the first two months, Ella mostly looked at toys, because her body was not developed enough for her to reach for and hold them. Then, from 4 to 6 months of age, she started to hold on to toys and bring them to her mouth, which she did at every opportunity. In fact, one of the universal characteristics of 4- to 6-month-olds is their ability to look, grasp, and bring objects to their mouths.

From 6 to 8 months, Ella's play became more sophisticated. Her physical abilities progressed enough that she could explore toys in more meaningful ways. She learned to transfer objects from hand to hand, turn them over, give them to others, and finger, poke, and scratch at them. As Ella grew, she developed the ability to drop one object for another; and because she preferred novelty, she would often drop what she had for what was being offered. At the same time, she began to develop *object permanence*—knowing that an object exists even when not in sight. As a result of this milestone, she was able to pull the blanket off a favorite toy that was hidden but she wanted to find. So now, at 12 months, Ella likes the wrapping paper and box best!

During the next six months, Ella will begin to experiment with objects. She will scrunch the paper, it will make a noise, and she will change its shape when

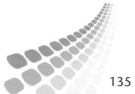

This article was first published in the May 2009 issue of *Young Children* in the column Rocking and Rolling: Supporting Infants, Toddlers, and Their Families.

Linda Gillespie, MS, has worked for ZERO TO THREE for the past 10 years and has been in the early childhood field for the past 35 years. Linda coordinates the writing of the Rocking and Rolling column in *Young Children*.

she pulls it apart. The box is a vessel she can fill, dump, and turn over and bang on. The paper and the box together provide her with endless opportunities to experiment and explore.

At 18 to 24 months, Ella will move into symbolic play, where a block will become a phone or a car. Her play will have more purpose and will take place alongside, and sometimes even with, others. Ella will begin to be able to solve problems through play, like putting a cube into a hole or nesting cups. And then the box will become a house or a hat or anything she wants it to be. The opportunities are as endless as her imagination!

Think About It

Watch how the babies in your care play. What does their play tell you about their development? How do they explore objects? What interests them? What is their environment like? Are there safe places on the floor where nonmobile and newly mobile infants can explore? Is there a variety of materials, not just plastic toys?

Try It

Offer one new object a week for infants younger than 12 months to explore. Here are some suggestions:

• Make a basket of objects, specifically those that appeal to touch, smell, and sound. Include materials with different textures—a cloth bag with spices in it, wooden items, a bell.

• Provide containers and a variety of materials for dumping and filling.

• Offer bowls of various unbreakable materials like plastic and stainless steel.

• Give infants containers that open and close, like plastic jars of different sizes.

Just be sure that anything you give a baby is large enough not to be swallowed and safe to put into their mouths. And don't forget the boxes!

Rocking and Rolling is written by infant/toddler specialists and contributed to *Young Children* by ZERO TO THREE, a nonprofit organization working to promote the health and development of infants and toddlers by translating research and knowledge into a range of practical tools and resources for use by the adults who influence the lives of young children.

Let's Get Messy! Exploring Sensory and Art Activities With Infants and Toddlers

Trudi Schwarz and Julia Luckenbill

It's raining lightly in the infant yard, and the babies are outside examining the wet grass and splashing in puddles. Aziz (17 months) picks up a ball and tosses it into a muddy puddle. He squeals in delight, bends down, and lifts the ball back up. He touches the mud, watching as it oozes onto his finger. He then drops the ball back into the puddle. Next, he walks over to a nearby shelf and grasps another ball, walks back, then drops that one into the puddle as well.

Fascinated by his messy discovery, Aziz continues to drop balls and other toys into the muddy water until it is time to go inside. Meanwhile, several other infants wobble over and imitate the game. Having observed the infants' interest, the next day the staff place a tub of water and balls in the indoor art/sensory area to extend the children's investigation.

Visitors who observe scenarios like the one described above often make surprised comments, such as, "You let them get that messy?" But these projects are commonplace in the infant and toddler classrooms where we teach. As infant/toddler teachers we take a child-centered, emergent approach, meaning that we observe the children at play, ask ourselves what they are interested in learning, and design developmentally appropriate curricula to meet and extend those interests. This curriculum development technique leads to "possibilities for the child to develop deeper understandings" of how the world works (Curtis & Carter 1996, 52). The activities in our classroom interest areas and our play yards change weekly, though the content in the areas remain in the same locations. When children arrive in the morning, they tend to beeline to their favorite areas to see what has changed. One of the preferred areas inside and outside is the art/sensory area.

We believe that art and sensory projects are integral to the curriculum, and that children develop key skills through these types of activities. This belief is supported by the Arts Education Partnership (TFCLA & Goldhawk 1998) and by the Infant/Toddler Environment Rating Scale—Revised (Harms, Cryer, & Clifford 2007). We provide art and sensory activities every day and give children ample time to explore them. Why? "Children must explore to know. A direct connection exists between sensory experiences and the development of creativity" (Miller 1999, 157). Smith and Goldhaber (2004) note, "Young

This article was first published in the September 2012 issue of *Young Children*.

Trudi Schwarz, MS, is the head teacher of the infant room at the Center for Child and Family Studies Laboratory School at the University of California, Davis.

Julia Luckenbill, MA, is a child development demonstration lecturer at the Center for Child and Family Studies Laboratory School at the University of California, Davis.

children actively test out their theories [ideas] many times before accommodating their own theories to knowledge gained from new experiences" (18–19). Through hands-on play, even infants are developing rudimentary theories (schemas) to explain their world. In other words, infants construct an idea of how things work in their heads, and then refine it over time through experience. For example, giving infants time to paint leads to them discovering that they have made marks on the paper. Over time, this understanding becomes more systematic and the children become capable of integrating new tools and media into their art.

Learning and Growing Through Art and Sensory Activities

Children benefit by engaging in hands-on exploration of materials. They add many vital "tools" to their school readiness toolbox through art/sensory play.

Motor Skill Development

• Poking, smashing, pinching, squeezing, cutting, and rolling playdough and real clay improves hand strength and fine motor skills.

• Grasping a crayon or marker and scribbling supports future writing and drawing skills. Toddlers initially use their whole arms to make scribble marks on paper. With practice they refine these skills and begin to make vague shapes. These early experiences support the ability to plan their artwork and draw things they know from their environment, usually during their preschool years (Cryer, Harms, & Riley 2004).

Social-Emotional Skills

• Painting together on a see-through easel or a shared piece of paper encourages children's ability to use materials together and supports prosocial interactions.

• Splashing side by side at the water table teaches toddlers about sharing spaces and leads to conversations about other children's feelings (e.g., if a child did not want to get wet).

Engaging in art and sensory play supports the emergence of children's new skills, while observing children's play provides vital information about children's developmental progress.

In this article, we share the experiences of the infant and toddler art/sensory program at our school. We begin with issues to consider when planning the curriculum, and provide ideas about where to find inexpensive, high-quality materials. Finally, we share some examples from our classrooms and offer suggestions for yours.

Planning a Curriculum

Visitors to our youngest classrooms are often surprised to discover that we have daily art and sensory activities, just as preschool classrooms do. However, there are essential differences between planning art/sensory activities for preschoolers and activities for infants and toddlers. Following are some things to consider when planning art/sensory activities.

Encourage Experimentation

Infants enjoy using their senses to learn and are very oral. It's best to design activities with this in mind. Infants love to gradually explore the texture, scent, taste, sight, and sound of the art materials. They often are messy in their use of the materials (e.g., crawling through paint). Projects must use materials that are washable, nontoxic, and do not contain small parts. Activities should be open-ended so that children have the time and space to construct their own understanding of the materials and their properties. Allow ample time for play and for cleanup.

A Note on Cultural Sensitivity

It is offensive in some cultures to use food as an art material—in particular, rice. Avoid this kind of activity, as you cannot be sure who may be offended by the waste of food. It is not always obvious if a child or their extended family have experienced food scarcity (Derman-Sparks & Olsen Edwards 2010). We have found that birdseed is a good nontoxic alternative to rice in a sensory table, and that fish tank gravel and cornstarch-based packing peanuts (they melt in your mouth) work just as well as beans and pasta for gluing on collages.

Some adults are concerned that infants and young toddlers might eat the art materials. While we don't encourage this behavior, we understand that tasting the materials is part of the children's exploratory process. We have found that after a small sample, children realize that the materials are not tasty, and teachers can then redirect them to a more appropriate use. For example, after an infant puts a (nontoxic) paint-covered finger in his mouth, a caregiver might say, "That doesn't taste so good. You can rub the paint on the paper instead." If you find that infants are eating large amounts of homemade playdough, switch to commercially made playdough or salt-free recipes, because an excess of salt is harmful to young children.

> Activities should be open-ended so that children have the time and space to construct their own understanding of the materials and their properties.

Supervise Exploration

As infants become toddlers, they use materials with more intentionality. They are less likely to eat the art materials, though they may still experiment by tasting them. Toddlers do not understand conservation of volume. They will squeeze a glue bottle until it is empty or shake all the colored sand out of the salt shaker and then demand more. They explore the nature of paint by decorating not only the paper, but also the table and themselves. Toddlers' explorations require close supervision from caregivers and enough space to be messy.

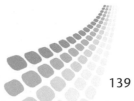

Affirm the Process

Infants and toddlers are *process* rather than *product* oriented. Placing cotton balls on the back of a die-cut sheep is less satisfying to them than finger painting. Coloring in a coloring book is less exciting than playing with playdough. Infants and toddlers want to feel the paint as it covers their fingers, smell the mint in the scented playdough, and taste the basil leaves in the tub on the table.

Use Culturally Diverse Materials

Use an antibias approach to all projects. Materials that reflect the cultures and backgrounds of the children you serve send a message that everyone is valued in the classroom (Derman-Sparks & Olsen Edwards 2010). For example, offer brown and tan playdough as well as pink shades, and provide training chopsticks to explore the playdough instead of plastic knives. Ask the children's parents to donate materials that reflect their backgrounds, such as origami or wrapping paper for use in collage. The more you keep the families in mind, the more inclusive and welcoming your program will be.

Make Accommodations for Special Needs

Art/sensory projects must be accessible to all children in your care and address a range of skills and abilities. This may mean making accommodations for children with special needs. For instance, you can place materials directly on the floor for children with mobility challenges or for those who cannot stand at a table. You can provide paintbrushes with extralarge handles for children with fine motor difficulty. To create them, wind self-adhering first aid wrap on the handle of the brush to make it easier to grasp.

Some children love the feel of gooey wet paint on their hands, while other children shy away from such slimy activities.

Modify Activities for Sensory Avoiders

Differences in temperament impact each child's response to art and sensory materials. For example, some children love the feel of gooey wet paint on their hands, while other children shy away from such slimy activities. If you have children in your care who avoid sensory experiences, you can include them by modifying sticky and gooey projects. For example, add brushes in the finger paint or cups with oobleck (a cornstarch and water mixture) so these children can explore the materials at their own pace and in a way that feels right to them. When sensory-avoidant children are exposed to art materials in a way that respects their unique temperaments, they may become more comfortable touching the materials as they become familiar with textures. Playing with finger paint, bubble water, and other sensory materials is part of a healthy "sensory diet" for all children. Engaging in these activities can help a child with sensory processing disorder (and children without the disorder as well) more easily interpret the environment (Arnwine 2007, 4).

Display Children's Artwork

Display the children's artwork at their eye level. This allows them to admire their creations and feel ownership of the classroom. Families also appreciate seeing their children's creations valued. Display 3-D art, such as playdough sculptures, in addition to paper collages and paintings. Children's art displays are an indicator of a high-quality classroom in the NAEYC accreditation standards and in both the Infant/Toddler and the Early Childhood Environment Rating Scale—Revised (ITERS-R/ECERS-R), which are tools used to assess the quality of early childhood learning environments (Harms, Clifford, & Cryer 2005; Harms, Cryer, & Clifford 2007).

Art and Sensory Activities in the Infant Room

It is wise to plan activities for young children in order to avoid chaotic transitions. When teachers plan curriculum based on their observations of children's interests, children's learning experiences are extended. Below is an example from our infant room.

Choosing the Activity

At snack time, we noticed 11-month-old Alice smearing her sweet potato on the table and gazing intently at the color. Other infants were also smearing their food while eating. Since the infants were clearly interested in spreading color, we decided that finger paint was a good extension.

Designing the Activity

We decided to introduce nontoxic foam paint in the art/sensory area. We placed the paint in a low bin on the floor and put wipes on a table near the paint.

Implementing the Activity

On the first day, several infants crawled or wobbled over to the paint bin. Some reached in, grasping and smearing the paint. Others poked it lightly with a finger or avoided it. We continued for several days with adults modeling that it was safe to touch the paint. Over the course of the week we saw more infants join in.

Changing the Activity

In response to the children's initial reaction to the project, we planned the following extensions:

1. We added round-ended paintbrushes (like shaving brushes), inviting infants to engage with the paint without smearing their fingers. Teachers allowed the children to explore the materials, and modeled using the brushes without requiring infants to try.

2. The following week, we observed the infants still showing interest in the paint. We changed the project very little, substituting finger paint for foam paint. The finger paint was more slippery than the foam paint. The infants continued to engage with the paint.

Sensory and Art Activities for Infants and Toddlers

Nontoxic material	Nontoxic items to place on or in the material	Surface	Tools	Ages and notes
Tempera paint, foam paint, finger paint	Colored sand and liquid soap	Paper, Plexiglass, wood, cardboard items, natural items, body parts, bubble wrap	Paintbrushes, stamps, sponges, plastic cars, plastic balls	Infants and toddlers
Watercolor block paint or liquid paint	None	Paper, coffee filters	Water, brushes, bottles for liquid watercolor	Toddlers
Contact paper	Colored sand, regular sand, natural materials, paper scraps, pictures from magazines, photos, recycled wrapping paper, pipe cleaners, tissue paper	Table or floor	Scotch tape or similar to affix contact paper to the table	Infants and toddlers
Stickers, tape	None	Paper or skin	None	Infants and toddlers
Construction paper, cardboard, tissue paper, newspaper, butcher paper, etc.	None	Paper can be used as a surface.	Tape to affix to the paper or materials to decorate it	Infants and toddlers. Crumpling, tearing, climbing into containers of crumpled paper, and making balls of paper.
Glue	None	Table with trays and paper or cardboard to hold collage	Glue bottles	Toddlers
Playdough, purchased or homemade. (*Note:* Limit how much playdough children eat due to the high salt content or make salt-free playdough, or purchase commercial playdough.)	Colored sand; liquid watercolor, food color, or extract (e.g., vanilla or peppermint); pipe cleaners; Popsicle sticks; leaves, sticks, shells, etc.	Table with trays to define each child's space, or a bin if a group of infants shares the playdough	Cookie cutters, cutting tools, baking tools, ceramic tools, tortilla presses, garlic presses, plastic toys as props	Infants and toddlers
Natural clay	Pipe cleaners, Popsicle sticks, nontoxic branches, water if clay is dry	Table or bin, trays optional	See above	Infants and toddlers. Clean up well after using clay to prevent dust buildup.
Water	Liquid watercolor or food color, soap, large ice blocks (but remove when they become smaller), cornstarch (oobleck), wool	Bins on or off a table. Towels taped to floor around this project.	Cups, funnels, bath toys, measuring cups, whisks, items that sink and float, eye droppers for toddlers	Infants and toddlers
Birdseed, sand, soil	Hidden toys or shells under the material. Water in the sand or soil.	Bins inside or outside to decrease mess. Water table.	Containers, sand mills, plastic vehicles or animals. Various sizes of tubes. Plastic beakers.	Infants and toddlers
Nontoxic leaves, pinecones, seedpods, flowers	Water, soil, clay	Table, bin, piles outside	Scissors (for toddlers only)	Infants and toddlers
Stamping ink/dot markers	None	Table with individual papers or butcher paper if this is a communal artwork. Wall with butcher paper.	Stamps for stamp pad. Both age groups are more likely to use hands.	Infants and toddlers
Crayons, colored pencils, markers, nontoxic oil pastels, chalk	None	Table with individual papers or butcher paper if this is a communal artwork. Wall with butcher paper.	None	Older infants and toddlers. Use chalk outside or with ventilation to prevent dust buildup.
Fabric	None	Can be connected into a "sensory blanket" with other materials such as bubble wrap for young infants to crawl over. Older children can use it on a table for collage.	Scissors (for toddlers only)	Infants and toddlers. Invites open-ended dramatic play and dance for toddlers.

3. We noticed that when we washed the paint off the infants' hands, they enjoyed the bubbles and water. We changed the paint to soapy water. More infants joined in this exploration—splashing, dumping items in the water, and even crawling in. The children engaged in this activity outside as well as inside.

4. We decided to explore oobleck. Oobleck looks a lot like paint and contains water, but it behaves differently than both substances. The infants were initially hesitant around this substance. They gradually joined in, especially after plastic cups were introduced so they could examine the substance without touching it, if they preferred to explore in this way.

Making a Record

To share the children's explorations with families and the wider community, we documented each infant art/sensory activity in our classroom photo essay, "Adventures in the Infant Room." The photo essays help parents and caregivers look back on infant and toddler learning. It also helps capture the range of process-based activities and models how they might be tried at home. Here is an excerpt from the infant room's oobleck documentation:

> Julia is observing Leo (15 months) and the oobleck. She has noticed that he avoids touching many sensory materials, using towels, cups, or brushes to engage with them instead. She locates cups as Leo joins the activity. Next she observes Leo touching the cups. She knows that he likes to enter play slowly.
>
> Julia notes Leo's gaze shifting from the cup to the oobleck. He lightly touches the oobleck. His finger comes back clean but wet. She responds by using parallel talk, a teaching technique where teachers describe aloud what children are doing in order to connect with them and expand their ideas. Julia says, "You touched it and now your finger got wet. Oobleck is wet." She imitates his action. Leo pushes his cup back into the oobleck, bottom first. Julia says, "If you want to pick up the oobleck, you can use the cup." She models this by filling her own cup with oobleck. She pours the oobleck out. "It comes out slowly," she comments. "Do you want to try?" Leo reaches out and grasps her cup and pours out the oobleck.
>
> The oobleck falls in puddles. Leo now appears comfortable with the substance. He grasps handfuls of it, pinches and squeezes it, and puts it back into his cup. Julia, still observing him, continues to facilitate his play, moving the oobleck back into the cups for further pouring. She narrates the action of the oobleck—how slowly it moves—and she talks about how Leo can pinch it to pick it up. She also steps back again, allowing him to feel autonomous in his exploration.

Art and Sensory Activities in the Toddler Room

We use the same techniques to design and expand curriculum in both the infant and toddler programs. Following is an example of a curriculum designed for older children.

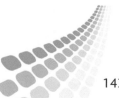

Choosing the Activity

Playdough was a passion in the toddler room. Each day children would ask for it by name, and they would crowd around the trays as we placed them on the tables, reaching for playdough and tools. We provided cookie cutters, butter knives, pizza cutters, and rolling pins to use with the dough. We noticed several toddlers putting globs of playdough on the butter knives and declaring them to be "Popsicles."

Designing and Implementing the Activity

We put out a range of materials, from Popsicle sticks and pipe cleaners to feathers and leaves, and then watched what the toddlers did and made. They excitedly created many "birthday cakes" by poking items into the playdough. They enjoyed singing "Happy Birthday" to themselves, their peers, and their caregivers.

Changing the Activity

In response to the children's initial reaction to the project, we planned the following extensions:

1. Noting the toddlers' interest in cakes, we set up a bakery shop. We added brown playdough, birthday candles, whisks, measuring cups, cupcake tins and wrappers, salt-filled shakers, and other baking tools to the trays. The toddlers jumped right in, making more cakes and cupcakes. They were particularly interested in the salt shakers and sometimes got into conflicts over taking turns using them.

2. We decided to make salt shaker art. We filled small glue bottles with about a tablespoon of glue apiece. We placed construction paper on trays, anticipating glue puddles. We placed colored sand in several recycled spice shakers and taped over some of the holes to make the sand come out slowly. The toddlers made small glue lakes and shook all the sand out into colorful piles. We scooped the excess sand up, refilled the spice containers, and repeated the process. The toddlers did not understand that the glue made the sand stick, or that if they used too much glue the sand would fall off, but they loved the process. As expected, this was a developmentally appropriate outcome. Although children at this age do not carefully use glue, they do enjoy the experience of emptying, squeezing, and making a mess.

3. We added food coloring to the glue in the bottles after observing that the toddlers enjoyed using the glue puddles as paint.

4. The toddlers did not want to stop using shakers—it was so much fun! We took the activity outside to the dramatic play table beside the sandbox. Here the toddlers could make a mess using filled shakers without getting the classroom salty or sandy. They could also refill the shakers with sand. We knew the toddlers would "ruin" the playdough with the sand, but we accepted this as part of the process. This project included the initial playdough and accessories, salt shakers filled with various substances, and glue with and without food color.

Making a Record

To share the children's explorations with parents and visitors to our school, we documented each toddler art/sensory activity in the classroom in a photo essay, "Adventures in the Toddler Room." Here is an excerpt from the toddler room's glue-and-sand activity:

> We introduced glue-and-sand painting. This was a direct extension of last week's bakery shop project. We noticed that the toddlers loved using shakers and enjoyed decorating with sand.
>
> Peter is using both hands to squeeze out colored glue from the bottle. He has placed his sand down before the glue. This shows us that he does not understand that the glue will make the sand stick to the paper, but that he is testing out the properties of both materials on the paper.
>
> Andy and Joo are engaging in a similar process, testing the materials without being told how to use them by an adult. They are developing strong fine motor skills as they handle the tools.

Conclusion

We have found that the art and sensory investigations in the infant and toddler classrooms are some of the most exciting that we provide. Well-planned projects that include time for exploration and a way to control—or at least contain—the mess allow everyone to relax and enjoy the process. We encourage you to try art and sensory activities with the infants and toddlers in your care. There is nothing like seeing a child realize that she has caused a mark on a paper, or watching a toddler discover for himself that mixing blue and red makes purple. While art explorations with infants and toddlers are certainly more work for caregivers, they have a strong positive impact on young children's development and learning.

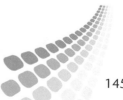

More, All Gone, Empty, Full:
Math Talk Every Day in Every Way

Jan Greenberg

Will feeds Maya, an 8-month-old in his care. He pauses for a moment and Maya signs "more." Will laughs. "You want more? Okay, here it comes!" He continues feeding her and when the bowl is empty, Will says and signs, "All gone. Maya ate her food. All gone." Maya looks at him and smiles.

Will knows that the development of math concepts and skills begins in the first years of life. In fact, from the moment they are born, children begin to construct ideas about mathematics through everyday routines, experiences, and, most importantly, caring interactions with trusted adults. A key aspect of these interactions involves language—how we talk math with infants and toddlers. It's easier than you think. You might be talking math more than you realize! Being aware of early mathematical concepts helps you be more thoughtful and intentional about using these concepts in everyday experiences and interactions with infants and toddlers.

Where's the Math?

Math is everywhere! Mathematics is "a way of describing the world—a way of thinking, knowing, and problem-solving" (VECDAP 2008, 83). You likely use math and math language all the time but may not be aware of it. For example, when you do laundry and wash clothes separately based on color, you're using the math concepts of sorting and classifying. You also use math concepts when you keep score during sporting events and explain how much your team is ahead or behind (number and operations), or give someone verbal directions to get from one place to another (spatial relationships). As a teacher or caregiver, you likely play games and sing songs that use numbers and counting, use comparison words such as *big* and *little* (measurement), and explain the order of everyday routines and experiences (patterns). In the short vignette in the beginning, Will builds on Maya's concept of *more* by feeding her more food. He also introduces a new math concept, "all gone." Math is all around us; math talk brings it out and makes it known.

Infants and toddlers are natural mathematicians. Even without adult support, we see infants and toddlers using math concepts to make sense of their world. For example, infants signal they want *more* food, as Maya does. *More* is one of the first math concepts that children construct (Ginsburg, Lee, & Boyd 2008). They tell us—often dramatically—that they know the difference between familiar and unfamiliar adults (sorting and classifying). Toddlers try to climb into boxes of various sizes (spatial relationships) and say words that are repeated in stories you read aloud or songs you sing (patterns) (Greenberg & Bickart 2008). An important role for teachers and other caregivers is to make the math that occurs in daily life concrete and visible to children. This is done through math talk.

Components of Math

One way to recognize and talk about math opportunities is to know what math involves. Here are brief descriptions of five math components and examples of talking math for each (Greenberg & Bickart 2008; VECDAP 2008).

Number and operations—understanding the concept of number, quantity, order, ways of representing numbers, one-to-one correspondence, and counting.

- "You have *two* eyes, and so does your bear. Let's *count: 1, 2*."
- "I have *more* crackers than you do. See, I have *three* and you have *two*. I'm going to eat *one* of mine. Now I have *the same as* you!"
- "That's the *third* time I've heard you say 'mama.' You've said 'mama' *three times*!"

Shapes and spatial relationships (geometry)—recognizing, naming, comparing, and contrasting objects based on their geometric appearance; understanding the physical relationship (i.e., direction and position) between self and objects, or between two or more objects, in one's environment.

- "Look, Jason went *under* the climber and Aliyah is *on top*!"
- "You're sitting *next to* Carlos."
- "Some of the crackers we have today are *square*, and some are *round*."

Measurement—determining qualities such as size, weight, quantity, volume, and time, and using the appropriate tools to do so.

- "Moving that stool is hard. It's *heavy*."
- "You took a *long* nap today!"
- "Let's *count how many steps* it takes to reach the playground."

Patterns, relationships, and change (building blocks of algebra)—recognizing (seeing the relationships that make up a pattern) and/or creating repetitions of objects, events, colors, lines, textures, and sounds; understanding that things change over time and that change can be described using math words.

- "Marcus has stripes on his shirt—white, blue, white, blue, white blue."
- "I put the blocks in the bucket, you dump them out. I put the blocks back in the bucket, you dump them out!"
- "Our plant looks *taller* today. I think it grew overnight."

This article was first published in the May 2012 issue of *Young Children* in the column Rocking and Rolling: Supporting Infants, Toddlers, and Their Families.

Jan Greenberg, BS, has worked for ZERO TO THREE for almost three years and has been in the early childhood field for more than 30 years, including time spent as a teacher, training/technical assistance provider, training manager, and resource developer.

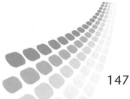

Collecting and organizing information (data collection and analysis)— gathering, sorting, classifying, and analyzing information to help make sense of what is happening in the environment.

• "You put the big lid on the big pot and the small lid on the small pot."

• "You always smile when your mom sings to you!"

• "Let's put the dolls in the basket and the balls in the box."

Involving Families

Families play an important role in helping infants and toddlers learn about math. They are their children's first teachers. As you become more aware of and intentional about talking math throughout the day, share your knowledge with families and ask them what math they see happening at home.

If needed, help them identify opportunities during their daily routines and experiences to talk math with their children. For example, diapering, meal and bath times, walks around the neighborhood, and shopping trips are ideal times to count, point out shapes and sizes, talk about patterns, and describe how things are the same and different. Encourage families to use their home language. When families speak in their home language, they strengthen their relationships with their children and are more likely to have meaningful conversations using rich, descriptive words (OHS 2008).

Putting It Together

Math is all around us. There are countless opportunities during the day for children to hear new math words and deepen their understanding of math concepts. The more we talk math and share our enjoyment of the experience with infants and toddlers, the better chance they have to build a positive attitude toward math learning and learning in general.

Think About It

• Reflect on your daily routines and activities. Identify the math-related content, skills, and language involved.

• Reflect on your own feelings about math.

This last point is especially important. If your experiences with math were not so great, you may unintentionally avoid focusing on math with young children. If this is the case, you may have to exert extra effort to ensure you provide children with many opportunities to explore math.

Try It

• Identify opportunities during your program's daily routines and experiences when you might use math talk.

• Observe a coteacher or colleague for a period of time, and note when she uses math talk and what words she uses. Then ask her to observe you so that you have a sense of what you're already doing and what you might improve.

• Make a list of math talk words and phrases. Post some on the walls to help you notice math talk opportunities. Rotate the words and phrases so they stay fresh.

• Plan a way to share with colleagues and families what you've learned about math talk and play. You can learn much more about math talk and strategies by doing this!

All gone, more, empty, full, and many more math words you use will enrich the everyday math experiences that infants and toddlers enjoy. You will be surprised at how much they know and can learn. Your math talk today can help the young children in your care get ready to be successful in math as they get older.

Rocking and Rolling is written by infant/toddler specialists and contributed to *Young Children* by ZERO TO THREE, a nonprofit organization working to promote the health and development of infants and toddlers by translating research and knowledge into a range of practical tools and resources for use by the adults who influence the lives of young children.

References

Abbott, L., & A. Langston, eds. 2005. *Birth to Three Matters: Supporting the Framework of Effective Practice*. London: Open University Press.

Arnwine, B. 2007. *Starting Sensory Integration Therapy: Fun Activities That Won't Destroy Your Home or Classroom*. Arlington, TX: Future Horizons.

Aronson, S.S. 2002. *Model Child Care Health Policies*. 4th ed. Elk Grove Village, IL: American Academy of Pediatrics.

Aronson, S.S., ed. 2012. *Healthy Young Children: A Manual for Programs*. 5th ed. Washington, DC: NAEYC.

August, D., & T. Shanahan, eds. 2006. *Developing Literacy in Second-Language Learners. Report of the National Literacy Panel on Language-Minority Children and Youth*. Mahwah, NJ: Erlbaum.

Bauer, P., & T. Pathman. 2008. "Memory and Early Brain Development." *Encyclopedia on Early Childhood Development*, eds. R.E. Tremblay, M. Boivin, & R DeV Peters, 1–5. Montreal: Centre of Excellence for Early Childhood Development and Strategic Knowledge Cluster on Early Child Development. www.child-ency-clopedia.com/documents/Bauer-PathmanANGxp.pdf.

Berk, L.E. 2012. *Child Development*. 9th ed. Upper Saddle River, NJ: Pearson.

Bjorklund, D.F. 2011. *Children's Thinking: Cognitive Development and Individual Difference*. 5th ed. Belmont, CA: Cengage Learning.

Blum, L. 1987. "Particularity and Responsiveness." Chap. 7 in *The Emergence of Morality in Young Children,* eds. J. Kagan & S. Lamb, 306–37. Chicago: University of Chicago Press.

Bowman, B.T., S. Donovan, & M.S. Burns. 2000. *Eager to Learn: Educating Our Preschoolers*. Washington, DC: National Academies Press.

Brazelton, T.B., & J. Sparrow. 2006. *Touchpoints Birth to Three*. 2nd ed. Reading, MA: Da Capo.

Brazelton, T.B., & S.I. Greenspan. 2000. *The Irreducible Needs of Children: What Every Child Must Have to Grow, Learn, and Flourish*. Cambridge, MA: Da Capo.

Bredekamp, S., ed. 1986. *Developmentally Appropriate Practice*. Washington, DC: NAEYC.

Bredekamp, S., ed. 1987. *Developmentally Appropriate Practice in Early Childhood Programs Serving Children From Birth Through Age 8*. Exp. ed. Washington, DC: NAEYC.

Bredekamp, S., & C. Copple, eds. 1997. *Developmentally Appropriate Practice in Early Childhood Programs Serving Children From Birth Through Age 8*. Rev. ed. Washington, DC: NAEYC.

Bronfenbrenner, U., & P.A., Morris. 2006. "The Bioecological Model of Human Development." In *Theoretical Models of Human Development,* ed. R.M. Lerner, 793–828. Vol. 1 of *Handbook of Child Psychology,* 6th ed., eds. W. Damon & R.M. Lerner. New York: Wiley.

Bronson, P., & A. Merryman. 2009. *NurtureShock: New Thinking About Children*. New York: Twelve.

Bruner, J. 1985. *Child's Talk: Learning to Use Language*. New York: Norton.

CDE (California Department of Education). 2009. *California Infant/Toddler Learning & Development Foundations*. Sacramento: CDE.

Cole, M., S. Cole, & C. Lightfoot. 2005. *The Development of Children*. 5th ed. New York: Worth Publishers.

Copple, C., & S. Bredekamp. 2006. *Basics of Developmentally Appropriate Practice: An Introduction for Teachers of Children 3 to 6*. Washington, DC: NAEYC.

Copple, C., & S. Bredekamp, eds. 2009. *Developmentally Appropriate Practice in Early Childhood Programs Serving Children From Birth Through Age 8*. 3rd ed. Washington, DC: NAEYC.

Cryer, D., T. Harms, & C. Riley. 2004. *All About the ITERS-R*. Lewisville, NC: Pact House.

Curtis, D. & M. Carter. 1996. *Reflecting Children's Lives: A Handbook for Planning Child-Centered Curriculum*. St. Paul, MN: Redleaf.

DaRos-Voseles, D. 2009. "Caring and Caregiving: It All Starts Here." Paper presented at the International Infant/Toddler Conference in Tulsa, Oklahoma.

Derman-Sparks, L., & J. Olsen Edwards. 2010. *Anti-Bias Education for Young Children and Ourselves*. Washington, DC: NAEYC.

Doidge, N. 2007. *The Brain That Changes Itself*. New York: Penguin.

Eisenberg, N. 1992. *The Caring Child*. Cambridge, MA: Harvard University Press.

Eisenberg, N., & P.H. Mussen. 1989. *The Roots of Prosocial Behavior in Children*. Cambridge: Cambridge University Press.

Elicker, J., & M.B. McMullen. 2013. "Infants and Toddlers. Appropriate and Meaningful Assessment in Family-Centered Programs." *Young Children* 68 (3).

Elicker, J., C.A. Fortner-Wood, & I.C. Noppe. 1999. "The Context of Infant Attachment in Family Child Care." *Journal of Applied Developmental Psychology* 20 (2): 319–36.

Elkind, D. 2007. *The Power of Play: Learning What Comes Naturally*. Reading, MA: Da Capo.

Epstein, A.S. 2007. *The Intentional Teacher: Choosing the Best Strategies for Young Children's Learning*. Washington, DC: NAEYC.

Erikson, E. 1950. *Childhood and Society*. New York: Norton.

Field, T. 2007. *The Amazing Infant*. Malden, MA: Blackwell Publishing.

Flavell, J., & Hartman, B. 2004. "What Children Know About Mental Experiences" Research in Review. *Young Children* 59 (2): 102–109.

Fort, P., & R. Stechuk. 2008. "The Cultural Responsiveness and Dual Language Education Project." *Zero to Three* 29 (1): 24–28.

Fulghum, R. [1986] 2004. *All I Really Need to Know I Learned in Kindergarten*. New York: Ballantine.

Ginsburg, H.P, J.S. Lee, & J.S. Boyd. 2008. "Mathematics Education for Young Children: What It Is and How to Promote It." *Social Policy Report* 22 (1): 3–23.

Gonzalez-Mena, J. 2009. *Fifty Strategies for Communicating and Working With Diverse Families*. 2nd ed. Boston: Pearson.

Goodwyn, S.W., L.P. Acredolo, & C. Brown. 2000. "Impact of Symbolic Gesturing on Early Language Development." *Journal of Nonverbal Behavior* 24 (2): 81–103.

Gopnik, A. n.d. "Creating Healthy Connections: Nurturing Brain Development From Birth to Three." Podcast. 21 min. www.zerotothree.org/about-us/funded-projects/parenting-resources/podcast/creating-healthy-connections.html.

Gordon, M. 2009. *Roots of Empathy: Changing the World Child by Child*. New York: The Experiment.

Greenberg, J., & T.S. Bickart. 2008. *Math Right From the Start: What Parents Can Do in the First Five Years*. Washington, DC: Teaching Strategies.

Harms, T., R.M. Clifford, & D. Cryer. 2005. *Early Childhood Environment Rating Scale Revised*. New York: Teachers College Press.

Harms, T., D. Cryer, & R.M. Clifford. 2007. *Infant/Toddler Environment Rating Scale Revised Edition*. New York: Teachers College Press.

Hart, B., & T. Risley. 1995. *Meaningful Differences in Everyday Parenting and Intellectual Development in Young American Children*. Baltimore: Brookes.

Hirsh-Pasek, K., R.M. Golinkoff, L.E. Berk, & D.G. Singer. 2009. *A Mandate for Playful Learning in Preschool: Presenting the Evidence*. New York: Oxford University Press.

Hirsh-Pasek, K., R.M. Golinkoff, & D. Eyer. 2003. *Einstein Never Used Flash Cards: How Our Children Really Learn—And Why They Need to Play More and Memorize Less*. Emmaus, PA: Rodale.

Honig, A.S. 1982. *Playtime Learning Games for Young Children*. Syracuse, NY: Syracuse University Press.

Honig, A.S. 1997. "Infant Temperament and Personality: What Do We Need to Know?" *Montessori Life* 9 (3): 18–21.

Honig, A.S. 2002. *Secure Relationships: Nurturing Infant/Toddler Attachment in Early Care Settings*. Washington, DC: NAEYC.

Honig, A.S. 2004. "Twenty Ways to Boost Your Baby's Brain Power." *Scholastic Parent and Child* 11 (4): 55–56.

Honig, A.S. 2007. "Oral Language Development." *Early Child Development and Care* 177 (6): 581–613.

Honig, A.S. 2009. "Stress and Young Children." In *Informing Our Practice: Useful Research on Young Children's Development*, eds. E. Essa & M.M. Burnham, 71–88. Washington, DC: NAEYC.

Honig, A.S. 2010. *Little Kids, Big Worries: Stress-Busting Tips for Early Childhood Classrooms*. Baltimore: Brookes.

Honig, A.S., & M. Shin. 2001. "Reading Aloud to Infants and Toddlers in Childcare Settings: An Observational Study." *Early Childhood Education Journal* 28 (3): 193–97.

Hyson, M. 2004. *The Emotional Development of Young Children: Building an Emotion-Centered Curriculum*. 2nd ed. New York: Teachers College Press.

Hyson, M. 2008. *Enthusiastic and Engaged Learners: Approaches to Learning in the Early Childhood Classroom*. New York: Teachers College Press.

Jalongo, M.R. 2007. *Early Childhood Language Arts*. 4th ed. New York: Pearson.

Jennings, J. 2005. "Inclusion Matters." Chap. 8 in *Birth to Three Matters: Supporting the Framework of Effective Practice*, eds. L. Abbott & A. Langston, 89–104. London: Open University Press.

Johnson, J.A., & T.A. Johnson. 2006. *Do-It-Yourself Early Learning: Easy and Fun Activities and Toys From Everyday Home Center Material*. St. Paul, MN: Redleaf.

Kaplan, L. 1978. *Oneness and Separateness: From Infant to Individual*. New York: Simon & Schuster.

Katz, L.G., & S.C. Chard. 2000. *Engaging Children's Minds: The Project Approach*. 2nd ed. Norwood, NJ: Ablex.

Katz, L.G., & D.E. McClellan. 1997. *Fostering Children's Social Competence: The Teacher's Role*. Washington, DC: NAEYC.

Keyser, J. 2006. *From Parents to Partners: Building a Family-Centered Early Childhood Program*. St. Paul, MN: Redleaf; Washington, DC: NAEYC.

Klein, P.S., R.R. Kraft, & C. Shohet. 2010. "Behaviour Patterns in Daily Mother–Child Separations: Possible Opportunites for Stress Reduction." *Early Child Development and Care* 180: 387–96.

Kohlberg, L. 1971. *Stages of Moral Development as a Basis of Education*. Cambridge, MA: Harvard University Press.

Kreader, J.L., D. Ferguson, & S. Lawrence. 2005. "Infant and Toddler Child Care Arrangements." *Child Care and Early Education Research Connections: Research-to-Policy Connections* 1: 1–5. www.nccp.org/publications/pdf/text_628.pdf.

Kuhl, P. "The Linguistic Genius of Babies." Filmed October 2010. TED video, 10:18. Posted February 2011. www.ted.com/talks/patricia_kuhl_the_linguistic_genius_of_babies.html.

Lally, J.R., & P.L. Mangione. 2008. "The Program for Infant Toddler Care." In *Approaches to Early Childhood Education*, 5th ed., eds. J.P. Roopnarine & J.E. Johnson. Upper Saddle River, NJ: Pearson.

Landry, S.H. 2008. "Effective Early Childhood Programs: Turning Knowledge Into Action." Chap. 4 in *Investing in Early Childhood Development: Evidence to Support a Movement for Educational Change*, eds. A.R. Tarlov & M.P. Debbink, 67–84. New York: Palgrave Macmillan.

Lee, G.Y.C. "Fetal and Newborn Auditory Processing of the Mother's and Father's Voice." Master's thesis, Queen's University, Kingston, Ontario, Canada, 2010. http://qspace.library.queensu.ca/bitstream/1974/6027/1/Lee_Grace_Y_201009_MSc.pdf.

Lonigan, C.J. 2006. "Development, Assessment, and Promotion of Preliteracy Skills." *Early Education and Development* 17 (1): 91–114.

MacDonald, S. 2001. *Block Play*. Beltsville, MD: Gryphon House.

Mann, M.B., & R.N. Carney. 2008. "Building Positive Relationships in the Lives of Infants and Toddlers in Child Care." In *Enduring Bonds: The Significance of Interpersonal Relationships in Young Children's Lives,* ed. M. R. Jalongo, 147–57. New York: Springer.

Marotz, L.R., & K.E. Allen. 2012. *Developmental Profiles: Prebirth Through Adolescence*. Stamford, CT: Cengage Learning.

McAfee, O., D.J. Leong, & E. Bodrova. 2004. *Basics of Assessment: A Primer for Early Childhood Educators*. Washington, DC: NAEYC.

McClelland, M.M., A.C. Acock, & F.J. Morrison. 2006. "The Impact of Kindergarten Learning-Related Skills on Academic Trajectories at the End of Elementary School." *Early Childhood Research Quarterly* 21 (4): 471–90.

McMullen, M.B. 1999. "Achieving Best Practices in Infant and Toddler Care and Education." Research in Review. *Young Children* 54 (4): 69–76.

McMullen, M.B., & S. Dixon. 2006. "Building on Common Ground: Unifying the Practices of Infant Toddler Specialists Through a Mindful, Relationship-Based Approach." Research in Review. *Young Children* 61 (4): 46–52.

McMullen, M.B., & S. Dixon. 2009. "In Support of a Relationship-Based Approach to Practice With Infants and Toddlers in the United States." Chap. 8 in *Participatory Learning and the Early Years,* eds. D. Bethelsen, J. Brownlee, & E. Johansson. London: Routledge.

McMullen, M.B., J.M. Addleman, A.M. Fulford, S. Moore, S.J. Mooney, S.S. Sisk, & J. Zachariah. 2009. "Learning to Be *Me* While Coming to Understand *We*. Encouraging Prosocial Babies in Group Settings." *Young Children* 64 (4): 20–28. www.naeyc.org/files/yc/file/200907/McMullenWeb709.pdf.

Miller, K. 1999. *Simple Steps: Developmental Activities for Infants, Toddlers, and Two-Year-Olds*. Beltsville, MD: Gryphon House.

Montagu, A. 1971. *Touching: The Human Significance of the Skin*. New York: Harper & Row.

MSDE (Maryland State Department of Education) & JHUSE (Johns Hopkins University School of Education). 2010. *Healthy Beginnings: Supporting Development and Learning From Birth Through Three Years of Age*. http://cte.jhu.edu/onlinecourses/HealthyBeginnings/HBFINAL.pdf.

NAEYC. 1996. "Developmentally Appropriate Practice in Early Childhood Programs Serving Children From Birth Through Age 8." Position statement. In *Developmentally Appropriate Practice in Early Childhood Programs*, rev. ed., eds. S. Bredekamp & C. Copple, 3–30. Washington, DC: NAEYC.

NAEYC. 2009. "Developmentally Appropriate Practice in Early Childhood Programs Serving Children Birth Through Age 8." Position statement. Washington, DC: NAEYC. www.naeyc.org/positionstatements/dap.

NAEYC & NAECS/SDE (National Association of Early Childhood Specialists in State Departments of Education). 2003. "Early Childhood Curriculum, Assessment, and Program Evaluation: Building an Effective, Accountable System in Programs for Children Birth Through Age 8." Joint position statement. Washington, DC: NAEYC. www.naeyc.org/files/naeyc/file/positions/CAPEexpand.pdf.

Nemeth, K.N. 2012. *Many Languages, Building Connections: Supporting Infants and Toddlers Who Are Dual Language Learners*. Lewisville, NC: Gryphon House.

Noddings, N. 2003. *Caring: A Feminine Approach to Ethics and Moral Education*. 2nd ed. Berkeley: University of California Press.

Notari-Syverson, A. 2006. "Everyday Tools of Literacy." In *Learning to Read the World: Language and Literacy in the First Three Years,* eds. S.E. Rosenkoetter & J. Knapp-Philo, 61–80. Washington, DC: ZERO TO THREE.

NRC (National Research Council). 2001. *Eager to Learn: Educating Our Preschoolers*. Washington, DC: National Academies Press. www.nap.edu/openbook.php?record_id=9745&page=1.

NSCDC (National Scientific Council on the Developing Child). 2004. *Young Children Develop in an Environment of Relationships. Working Paper #1*. Cambridge, MA: NSCDC, Center on the Developing Child at Harvard University. http://developingchild.harvard.edu/index.php/resources/reports_and_working_papers/working_papers/wp1/.

Odom, S.L., ed. 2002. *Widening the Circle: Including Children With Disabilities in Preschool Programs.* New York: Teachers College Press.

OHS (Office of Head Start). 2008. "A Family Note on Finding the Math." Washington, DC: Health and Human Services/Administration for Children and Families. http://eclkc.ohs.acf.hhs.gov/hslc/tta-system/teaching/eecd/Curriculum/Planning/Family_note_math_all_3_10_08_final.pdf.

Paley, V. 2004. *A Child's Work.* Chicago: University of Chicago Press.

Parlakian, R. 2004. "Early Literacy and Very Young Children." *Zero to Three* 25 (1): 37–44.

Perry, B.D., L. Hogan, & S. Marlin. 2000. "Curiosity, Pleasure and Play: A Neurodevelopmental Perspective." *HAAEYC Advocate.* http://caeyc.org/main/caeyc/proposals/pdfs/handouts%20creativity%20and%20Play.pdf.

Piaget, J. 1962. *Play, Dreams and Imitation in Childhood.* New York: Norton.

Piaget, J., & B. Inhelder. 1969. *The Psychology of the Child.* New York: Basic.

Pianta, R.C., W.S. Barnett, L.M. Justice, & S.M. Sheridan, eds. 2012. *Handbook on Early Childhood Education.* New York: Guilford.

Quann, V., & C.A. Wien. 2006. "The Visible Empathy of Infants and Toddlers." *Young Children* 61 (4): 22–29. www.naeyc.org/files/yc/file/200607/Quann709BTJ.pdf

Raikes, H.H., & C.P. Edwards. 2009. *Extending the Dance in Infant and Toddler Caregiving: Enhancing Attachment & Relationships.* Baltimore: Brookes; Washington, DC: NAEYC.

Ramey, C.T., & S.L. Ramey. 1999. *Right From Birth: Building Your Child's Foundation for Life.* New York: Goddard Press.

Riley, D., R.R. San Juan, J. Klinkner, & A. Ramminger. 2008. *Social and Emotional Development: Connecting Science and Practice in Early Childhood Settings.* St. Paul, MN: Redleaf; Washington, DC: NAEYC.

Rosenkoetter, S.E., & J. Knapp-Philo, eds. 2006. *Learning to Read the World: Language and Literacy in the First Three Years.* Washington, DC: ZERO TO THREE.

Sandall, S., M.L. Hemmeter, B.J. Smith, & M.E. McLean, eds. 2005. *DEC Recommended Practices: A Comprehensive Guide for Practical Application in Early Intervention/Early Childhood Special Education.* Longmont, CO: Sopris West, and Missoula, MT: Division for Early Childhood, Council for Exceptional Children.

Schweinhart, L.J., & D.P. Weikart. 1997. "*Lasting Differences: The High/Scope Preschool Curriculum Comparison Study Through Age 23.*" Monographs of the High/Scope Educational Research Foundation, vol. 12. Ypsilanti, MI: High/Scope Press.

Shonkoff, J.P., & D.A. Phillips, eds. 2000. *From Neurons to Neighborhoods: The Science of Early Child Development.* A report of the National Research Council. Washington, DC: National Academies Press. www.nap.edu/catalog.php?record_id=9824.

Shore, R. 1997. *Rethinking the Brain: New Insights Into Early Development.* New York: Families and Work Institute.

Shore, R. 2003. *Rethinking the Brain: New Insights Into Early Development.* Rev. ed. New York: Families and Work Institute.

Smith, D., & J. Goldhaber. 2004. *Poking, Pinching and Pretending: Documenting Toddlers' Explorations With Clay.* St. Paul, MN: Redleaf.

Stechuk, R.A., M.S. Burns, & S.E. Yandian. 2006. *Bilingual Infant/Toddler Environments: Supporting Language and Learning in Our Youngest Children.* Washington, DC: Academy for Educational Development.

Tabors, P.O. 2008. *One Child, Two Languages: A Guide for Early Childhood Educators of Children Learning English as a Second Language.* 2nd ed. Baltimore: Brookes.

Tough, P. 2009. *Whatever It Takes: Geoffrey Canada's Quest to Change Harlem and America.* New York: Mariner Books.

TFCLA (Task Force on Children's Learning and the Arts: Birth to Age Eight) & S. Goldhawk. 1998. *Young Children and the Arts: Making Creative Connections.* A report of the Task Force on Children's Learning and the Arts: Birth to Age Eight. Washington, DC: The Arts Education Partnership.

US Census Bureau. 2013. "Who's Minding the Kids? Child Care Arrangements: Spring 2011." Washington, DC: US Census Bureau. http://www.census.gov/prod/2013pubs/p70-135.pdf.

USDHHS (US Dept. of Health and Human Services). 2006. *Early Head Start Benefits Children and Families.* Washington, DC: Administration for Children and Families, Office of Planning, Research and Evaluation, Head Start Bureau. www.acf.hhs.gov/programs/opre/ehs/ehs_resrch/reports/dissemination/research_briefs/research_brief_overall.pdf.

VECDAP (Virginia's Early Childhood Development Alignment Project). 2008. *Milestones of Child Development: A Guide to Young Children's Learning and Development from Birth to Kindergarten.* Richmond: Office of Early Childhood Development, Virginia Department of Social Services. www.earlychildhood.virginia.gov/documents/milestones.pdf.

Vygotsky, L. [1934] 1986. *Thought and Language.* Trans. A. Kozulin. Cambridge, MA: MIT Press.

White, R., & V.L. Stoecklin. 2008. "Nurturing Children's Biophilia: Developmentally Appropriate Environmental Education for Young Children." White Hutchinson Leisure and Learning Group. www.white-hutchinson.com/children/articles/nurturing.shtml.

Winnicott, D.W. [1964] 1987. *The Child, the Family, and the Outside World.* New York: Perseus.

Yoshida, H. 2008. "The Cognitive Consequences of Early Bilingualism." *Zero to Three* 29 (2): 26–30.